LOVING BEGINS WITH ME

Loving Begins with Me

ELIZABETH SKOGLUND

Published in San Francisco by Harper & Row, Publishers

New York, Hagerstown, San Francisco, London

Loving Begins with Me. Copyright © 1979 by Elizabeth Skoglund. All rights reserved. Printed in the United States of America. No part of this book may be used or reproduced in any manner whatsoever without written permission except in the case of brief quotations embodied in critical articles and reviews. For information address Harper & Row, Publishers, Inc., 10 East 53rd Street, New York, NY 10022. Published simultaneously in Canada by Fitzhenry & Whiteside, Limited, Toronto.

FIRST EDITION

Designed by Jim Mennick

Library of Congress Cataloging in Publication Data
Skoglund, Elizabeth.
   LOVING BEGINS WITH ME.
     1. Christian life—1960-   2. Self-respect.
I. Title.
BV4501.2.S4757   248′.4   78–3364
ISBN 0–06–0673933–1

---

79 80 81 82 83   10 9 8 7 6 5 4 3 2 1

To Marilyn, whose friendship has been tested by the vicissitudes of life and whose relationship with me has nourished my self-esteem.

Contents

Foreword *ix*

1. Freeing Myself *1*
2. Growth Through Relationships *15*
3. I Am What I Do *30*
4. God Says I'm OK *44*
5. Growing Beyond Pain *58*
6. In Respect to Caring *71*
7. Survival Zone in a Changing World *87*

Foreword

Actually loving begins with God: "He first loved us" (I John 4:14). Unless we receive this input from outside, there will be no output from inside. This is precisely what Elizabeth Skoglund wants to say in her book. In the title, however, she points out the missing link in this love process initiated by God: me.

Often we forget that we need to have our own hands filled before we can pass on to others. We try to gain what we do not have by giving it out. Our failure in "loving me" is the result of this miscalculation.

No one loves himself or herself by nature. We have to learn it gradually in the process of life. This book is a good teacher, because it offers a positive concept of renouncing oneself, on creative unselfishness, and of constructive humility.

The many examples given in the book show that the

author writes out of practical experience. Through her personal testimony Elizabeth Skoglund witnesses to the fact that unless counseling is God-directed it isn't really client-centered.

For God created us "in His own image" and it is almost as if He would pat Himself on his back as a confirming gesture of divine self-acceptance when He states, looking at everything He had made, that "it was very good." (See Gen. 1:27 and 31)

So God felt pleased after he had made us, very pleased. Why can't we?

WALTER TROBISCH

CHAPTER 1

Freeing Myself

Michael looked intently at me as he said, "God could never love me. I'm not worth loving." Years of heroin addiction and jail had emphasized a self-image so nihilistic that it shut out even God. After all, how could God forgive a person who couldn't forgive him- or herself? How could God love someone who denigrated his or her own worth to God and humanity?

At another time, a young girl, Lisa, sat across from me looking a little wistful and lost. She had beautiful golden hair that fell in soft waves around her face and over her shoulders. Her eyes were deep blue and very expressive. Lisa was a very beautiful young girl, and when she spoke it was obvious that she was also intelligent. Still, one of her first statements was "I tried to overdose with pills because I'm ugly, stupid, and generally worthless."

People with self-esteem problems present as many

varying symptoms as there are different people. The root problem is a defective self-image; the presenting symptoms may differ vastly from person to person. A young girl sat and carved up her arms with a knife after being rejected by her boyfriend. A frustrated mother screamed at her four-year-old when her husband left her for another woman. A prominent business man kept his feelings of inadequacy bottled up and had an acute attack of peptic ulcers. Nor are these people unique, for all of us at one time or another really wonder if, at least at that moment, we *are* OK.

We humans are both very strong and very fragile. We have a strength that can survive the horror of Dachau and at the same time an ego that cannot tolerate a social slight nor rejection by one we love.

G. K. Chesterton once wrote,

> I felt and feel that life itself is as bright as the diamond but as brittle as the windowpane, and when the heavens were compared to the terrible crystal I can remember a shudder. I was afraid that God would drop the Cosmos with a crash.
>
> Remember, however, that to be breakable is not the same as to be perishable. Strike a glass, and it will not endure an instant; simply do not strike it, and it will endure a thousand years.[1]

We too are often breakable—but not perishable. We can endure much suffering, but, like the piece of glass windowpane, one sharp blow can almost do us in. How sharp that blow must be and how breakable we are depend largely on the strength of our self-image.

Self-esteem or a self-image is the view that one holds regarding oneself. It is the estimate one makes of one's worth. Sometimes that estimate is accurate, sometimes it is not. At times it is an unconscious attitude, for it is often too painful for people to face what they really think about themselves. The person who drinks excessively in order to "get courage" to fulfill obligations may only rarely admit that he or she does not like him- or herself. Even more rarely would the conceited person who claims to be better at everything than anybody else admit or even realize that conceit is an unrealistic cover for self-hate. Among Christians and non-Christians alike, the terms *low self-esteem, conceit, pride,* and *humility* have become confused and often distorted.

Low self-esteem is a feeling of worthlessness about oneself. Sometimes the feeling is conscious. At other times, it is very unconscious. Excessive drinking or pill taking, high levels of generalized anger, self-pity, excessive shyness, loudness at parties, depression, a martyrlike attitude and even many physical symptoms may in essence stem from a low self-image.

The advertising business is tuned in to this tendency to doubt ourselves and the temptation to meet the need for greater self-esteem by the use of superficial, easy answers. Prestige cars, clothes that sell more for their labels than for their quality, impressive homes, and the need for important friends who have the right jobs and social status are all feeble, ineffective ways to feel worth. The end result of using such things to elevate one's sense of worth is zero. Yet millions are spent every year on such things.

In spite of our attempts at easy answers, low self-esteem is a very real problem in our society and is probably the root factor in most people's emotional problems.

Frequently a low self-image or a good self-image are confused, respectively, with the biblical concepts of humility and pride. Humility is not groveling. It does not imply hating oneself or putting oneself down. True humility could best be defined as an absence of occupation with oneself, because people who truly like themselves do not have to keep evaluating their worth. They forget themselves in their task or in other people.

A few months ago, I visited a college professor who had done extensive research in a specific area of psychotherapy. I had done considerable reading on the subject but *he* was the expert. Expecting him to expound on his ideas, I was surprised to hear him asking me questions. When I gave answers, he seemed pleased with many of them and asked more. To me, he was the great scholar. Yet he himself acted with humility. He was confident, pleased with his work, anxious to learn more and eager to teach. He accepted himself so fully that he was free enough from himself to be involved in someone else's thinking.

In contrast, a false humility—when people tell you that they are not good at their jobs at all, when they are actually very proficient—is not humility at all but is just another manifestation of low self-esteem. Yet I have heard Bible teachers say such things as "If you don't think much of yourself, God is more free to help you." To the contrary, I have found that people who truly like themselves are more likely to be free and strong enough to trust God. When we trust ourselves, we find it easier to trust others, including God.

Conceit, too, is often misunderstood, particularly among Christians. The Psalms say that God hates a proud heart above all. In Psalm 131:1, we have a good definition of pride: "Lord, I am not proud and haughty . . . I don't pretend to 'know it all.' " Conceit actually reflects a *low* self-image. The teacher who says to his or her class, "I'm the best teacher you could have," is really saying "I hope I'm OK." He or she is trying to convince him- or herself and the class that he or she is at least adequate as a teacher. Such people brag, hoping above all that they will eventually believe themselves. It is accurate to conclude that if I'm sure I'm OK I don't have to tell you about it. If I'm sure I'm OK, I probably won't ever have to *think* about it. If I'm sure I'm OK, I will have a positive view of myself that will free me from pride and make me truly humble.

To have a good self-image is to feel comfortable with oneself, to be accepting of "who I am and why I am here." Put another way, to have good self-esteem is *to do the best with what we have* and improve where that is possible. We are not responsible for our intelligence level, but we *are* held to account for what we *do* with that intelligence. Thus retarded people may be of more worth to themselves and God than normal people if they handle themselves more responsibly within their potential. Of course, if brilliant people have the confidence to use their brilliance, not only for God and themselves but also for the betterment of humanity, their actual worth to *others* may be greater. People of all degrees of intelligence are worthwhile in that they are people who can be respected as being responsible for who they are and what they do. Whether they feel that worth and use it to its greatest potential depends on the level of their self-images.

There are at least two broad dimensions to a good self-image: a basic respect for *who* I am and a belief in the *why* of my existence. *Who* I am must be someone I respect, someone that has value even in those areas that no other person sees but only God knows. This idea is partly expressed by Robert Browning's suggestion that all he could never be, all that others ignored in him, this he was worth to God. The times when in private I have said to God, "In my innermost being, I relinquish my anger to you *even* though I have been misjudged and mistreated" or when I have acknowledged that "I want nothing but your will in my life in spite of my own cherished desires and hopes"—these times I have had worth to God and thus to myself as a person.

In addition to what people are inwardly, all that they do outwardly and the motivation therein is of extreme importance in developing strong positive feelings about who they are. For example, my Aunt Ruth worked for years in the interior of northern China. She taught little children to read and to know the love of Christ. She didn't bring her Western luxuries and American dress with her. She ate and lived like any other person in northern China. She witnessed the vicious killing of her close friend and physician during one of the Sino-Japanese wars. I have a photograph of her in a padded gown, looking very Chinese except for her white skin and brown hair. She was Christian, not only in her theology but also in her life. One of my happiest childhood memories is the time she took, while she was home, to cook Chinese food and tell stories to me, a five-year-old child. That in turn built my self-esteem, for how many people pay attention to children and really take them seriously?

My aunt had worth because of who she was and what she did. Her worth also affected my self-image because my roots go back to her and before her. What she was made me proud as a child, and pride in family contributes to a person's self-image.

The concept of family origin is popular in our society at this time. When Alex Haley's book *Roots* was published and then dramatized on television, we were ready for it. For years, people had been buying antiques—from clothes to furniture. Old pictures of anybody's family, just so long as they are old, are to be found on the walls of many homes. New furniture is antiqued to look old. We are overflowing with nostalgia and longing for the security that reaches back into the past.

The *why* of all of this looking back is obvious. We have had brutal breaks in family ties. We are dangerously independent. Our children grow up in nursery schools and with babysitters. Our old people go to convalescent homes. We are afraid of ties, of being committed or put out. But this leaves us with tremendous feelings of loneliness and emptiness. Sometimes we're not sure of who we really are. And so, even for those of us who try to be people we like and respect, there is a need to find where we come from. We are willing to suffer the degradation of what we find that is unpleasant in our genealogy for the sake of what we may find that will give us pride.

It is true that we find roots in our varied relationships in life, and these affect our feelings of self-worth. A good person who values me as such provides roots for me and increases my sense of self-worth. Still, we all have a sense of pride in finding out good things about our heritage.

I, for example, am proud of my aunt, who pioneered missionary work in northern China. That took guts. I take pride in my father, who emigrated to this country and worked full time at any job he could find until he became a licensed mechanical engineer. That took determination. There are countless other ways in which I feel good about my family past.

Of course, as with everyone, there are areas of mediocrity and failure. Yet even when we ourselves see faults in our families, there is truth in an old concept that, while we can criticize our own families, no one outside should. "I can say my husband is a lazy bum," commented one young woman, "but don't *you* call him that!" Why? Because our relatives reflect us—our taste, as in the case of this wife, or our very heritage and inherited characteristics! We need pride in our past. Perhaps that is why so many adopted children who deeply love their adoptive parents still seek out their natural parents.

Thus, while the *who* of our existence, in the sense of what kind of people we *are*, has a profound effect on our self-esteem, where we come from also plays an important part in understanding who we are. Perhaps we need to carefully reevaluate our current tendency toward isolation and indifference to the family unit. Children have the right to know their roots. Parents should tell them stories about their own childhoods and those of their grandparents. If possible, children should visit the geographical location of their heritage, especially if the family has come rather recently from another country.

For most of us, too, who we are or who we feel we are is affected by those whom we love and who love us back. Loving someone who loves me in return enhances my feelings of worth. Such feelings of worth are built from early childhood on. It is important to all of us that we love and are loved by worthwhile people. A little girl looked proudly up at her father as she rearranged the magazines in a doctor's waiting room. She loved him, respected him, and wanted his approval in return. Instead, he curtly responded, "Why can't you be that neat at home?" If there were a scientific instrument that recorded levels of self-esteem, it would have shot down very low as the child saw her father's response. All the bubbly happiness was gone, and she was near tears. He was a significant person in her life. Had she not loved him or not respected him, the effect would not have been so great, but because of her love and respect his response had a profound effect on her self-image.

In addition to the importance of *who* I am in the development of good self-esteem, I need to know the *why* of my existence. We are an identity-oriented society. Yet we also show our feelings of emptiness in a frantic rush of activity and an inability to comfortably handle quiet holidays and solitude. Some of this emptiness could be alleviated by the feelings of well-being that come from a deep sense of meaning. Here we can learn from psychiatrist Viktor Frankl's logotherapy. Frankl, who was threatened with his own feelings of emptiness while he was confined to concentration camps during World War II, says, "Everyone has his own specific vocation or mission in life; everyone must carry out a concrete assignment that demands fulfillment. Therein he cannot be replaced, nor can his life be repeated."[2] Frankl continues on a more personal level:

> Let me recall that which was perhaps the deepest experience I had in the concentration camp. The odds of surviving the camp were no more than one to twenty, as can easily be verified by exact statistics. It did not even seem possible, let alone probable that the manuscript of my first book, which I had hidden in my coat when I arrived at Auschwitz, would ever be rescued. Thus, I had to undergo and to overcome the loss of my spiritual child. And now it seemed as if nothing and no one would survive me; neither a physical nor a spiritual child of my own. So I found myself confronted with the question of whether under such circumstances my life was ultimately void of any meaning.
>
> Nor yet did I notice that an answer to this question with which I was wrestling so passionately was already in store for me, and that soon thereafter this answer would be given to me. This was the case when I had to surrender my clothes and in turn inherited the wornout rags of an inmate who had been sent to the gas chamber immediately after his arrival at the Auschwitz railway station. Instead of the many

pages of my manuscript, I found in a pocket of the newly acquired coat a single page torn out of the Hebrew prayer book, which contained the main Jewish prayer, *Shema Yisrael*. How should I have interpreted such a "coincidence" other than as a challenge to *live* my thoughts instead of merely putting them on paper?[3]

Frankl explains, "The question which beset me was, 'Has all this suffering, this dying around us, a meaning?' For if not, then ultimately there is no meaning to survival; for a life whose meaning depends upon such a happenstance—whether one escapes or not—ultimately would not be worth living at all."[4]

Frankl staunchly defends meaning in life even when someone is at the point of psychosis. Psychosis is just an extention of normalcy. To be suspicious now and then is not to be psychotic, but to walk around knowing that someone is going to literally kill you at any moment would usually be considered an indication of psychosis or insanity. Mental illness is a matter of degree, not kind. How depressed or suspicious or violent we become determines the degree of disturbance, not the fact that we experience these feelings. Thus Frankl's example of a psychotic person illustrates a basic principle for all of us: At any level of functioning, there is meaning. Frankl says,

I am reminded of a man of about sixty who was brought to me because of his auditory hallucinations lasting over many decades. I was facing a ruined personality. Now, his sister, who accompanied him, reported that sometimes he grew very excited; yet in the last moment he was always able to regain his self-control. I became interested in the

psychodynamics underlying the case, for I thought there was a strong fixation of the patient on his sister; so I asked how he managed to regain his self-control: 'For whose sake do you do so?' Thereupon there was a pause of some seconds, and then the patient answered: 'For God's sake. . . . '
An incurably psychotic individual may lose his usefulness but yet retain the dignity of a human being. This my psychiatric credo. Without it, I would not think it worthwhile to be a psychiatrist. For whose sake? Just for the sake of a damaged brain machine that cannot be repaired? If the patient were not definitely more, euthanasia would be justified.[5]

It is this purposefulness in human life that contributes a great sense of worth to an individual. To realize that worth, both of the *who* and the *why* of one's existence, is to have a good self-image.

Furthermore to be made in God's image is to be given a very sacred trust. Contrary to the thinking of many, to have a good self-image is consistent with the Scriptures. In Romans 12:3, we are told to make an honest estimate of ourselves. Furthermore, we read that God is a God of truth and that we are made in God's image. All imply that honesty about our good points as well as our bad is appropriate.

A strong biblical example is seen in the life of Joseph. He was the favorite of his father, but was not so defensive that he had to explain that position. When he was sold into Egypt by his own brothers, he did not waste his time bemoaning his rejection. Once in Egypt he became important on the staff of Potiphar who was close to Pharaoh, a position Joseph obtained because Potiphar noticed that everything he did succeeded and that God was with him in a special way. Yet when principle was involved, as when Potiphar's wife wanted to sleep with Joseph, he still valued himself and his position with God enough to turn the offer down and suffer the consequences of misunderstanding and jail. Later Joseph was justified, and Pharaoh put him in charge of all the land of Egypt, gave him his own signet ring to show authority, dressed him in beautiful clothing, and placed a golden chain about his neck. Despite all of that glory and prestige, Joseph did not take revenge on his brothers when they sought food from him. It is true that he held them off at first, for they had a lesson to learn. Joseph did not grovel to them. His final answer to his brothers concerning what they had done to him could be summarized in his words, "Don't be angry with yourselves that you did this to me, for God did it! He sent me here ahead of you to preserve your lives" (Genesis 45:5, TLB). What a delicate, balanced combination of wisdom, of a sense of good self-worth and of trust in Jehovah. Joseph was a man who knew his worth, accepted it, and used it. He did not ignore it, nor did he flaunt it.

It is true that we are to humble ourselves before God, for he is perfect. Yet, at the same time, every human being is to accept his or her own worth and improve it when that is possible. The extreme opposite of this ability is graphically illustrated in psychotic patients, who may altogether deny their own identities because they hate themselves so much. They then may imagine themselves to be someone else—great heroes, perhaps—because the thought of their own identities is so terrible.

A middle-aged man sat in my office for his last appointment. He no longer suffered from constant stomach upsets, and his business pressures were minimal compared to what they had been before, when he had compulsively worked most of his life away trying to be adequate at his job. He was about to take his first vacation in years. Before he left my office, John turned to me and said, "For the first time I feel free from myself or at ease with myself. I'm not trying to prove anything. I'm just doing the job I really *want* to do." To feel at ease with oneself! That is the essence of good self-esteem.

NOTES

1. G. K. Chesterton, *Orthodoxy* (New York: Lane, MCMXVIII), p. 101.
2. Viktor E. Frankl, *Man's Search for Meaning* (New York: Simon & Schuster, 1972), pp. 110–111.
3. Frankl (1972), pp. 116–117.
4. Frankl (1972), p. 117.
5. Frankl (1972), pp. 135–136.

CHAPTER 2

Growth Through Relationships

I have always heard people talk about those certain cycles of life when things go extremely well or poorly for a person. But I had not experienced the negative aspect of that observation until one memorable summer in my life. I changed my residence. Three of my closest friends moved to distant cities and drastically altered their lifestyles. Family death and sickness hit in bunches until I wondered when or *if* it would all stop? Could I take much more? When and how does a person make known the fact that he or she has had it? And under it all lay the nagging fear that maybe I just wasn't coping well. Would others do better in my place?

I developed a habit during that period of asking God for comfort. I was usually beyond specifying in what form that comfort should come, and so I found that God had a delightful way of answering my prayer in unexpected ways. During the toughest week of all, a friend called me daily just to see if things were any better and to tell me he admired my strength in handling the problems. Strength? That felt like the last word in my vocabulary. But my battered, bruised self-image responded like dry earth when it soaks up newly fallen rain. He never offered simplistic solutions like, "Why don't you just snap out of this?" He never made destructive statements like, "Maybe God isn't happy with you, and that's why you're suffering." He just stayed with me and let me heal at my own pace. I was OK, really OK. And I began to *feel* OK again. Relationships with people either damage or nourish our self-images. And my friend nourished mine.

The idea that other people affect our self-images has an obvious psychological validity when one considers the profound formative influence that parents have on small children. It is not unusual for me to have to work with a child of three in counseling sessions because the child has had three years of negative reinforcement from parents. Conversely, many children at that same age have a sturdy regard for their worth, because of positive parental influences. Nor are parents the only formative influence. Aunts, uncles, neighbors, even the clerk in the grocery store feed children images of who the children are and what they are worth.

It is an awesome truth that we mold our children into what they become. During our early years we form our images of ourselves from those closest to us. The self-image one develops continues to be reinforced throughout life by contacts with all sorts of people, particularly by those with whom we are most intimate.

Of course, our children have free will and exercise it. In a society where we have been trained all too well by the psychiatric community to believe that environment is the major influence on our lives, we need to be reminded that we too influence our own destiny. We choose who we will become. Many fine people have come from pathological backgrounds. Others function very poorly in spite of what appears to be a "good" family background.

We cannot avoid influencing others or being influenced. Yet we can make this choice if we so desire. For example, the friend who called me daily during a stressful period in my life *chose* to point out my strengths to me. He did not minimize my pain or act as though I were weak for feeling that pain. He did not denigrate me in any way. He viewed me as strong and translated that viewpoint to me. I grew in my self-esteem because a friend *chose* to reinforce it.

My will also played a part in this relationship, however, for I chose this friend originally. I constantly encounter people who have negative, nonsupportive friends. The negative attitudes rub off, and then these same people wonder why they are always struggling with their sense of worth. How else could they feel when they are constantly around people who support those negative feelings?

Helen and Joe saw me for marriage counseling for a number of months. Helen wanted a divorce but didn't want the responsibility of asking for one. So she played games. She tried to make Joe reject her. She demanded excessive money. He gave it to her. She left him with the sole responsibility for their young son. He accepted it. He did more and more housework. She went out more evenings. Finally she had an affair with Joe's best friend. Still Joe did not reject her. At that point, he made his first appointment with me.

"I feel like a nonperson," was his first comment to me. An already low self-image had been lowered because Joe chose to allow someone else to lower it. We choose our relationships. We choose to continue with them. And we decide, to a degree, the boundaries of those relationships. For example, Joe erased a big boundary when he assumed added household tasks and almost sole responsibility for his son. That choice lowered his view of himself because he viewed it as weakness, as a desperate inability to face losing Helen.

The therapeutic relationship in psychotherapy is one of those intimate relationships that can very deeply alter a person's self-image and build it into something stronger and more positive. It too becomes a choice of influence. When Joe chose to get counseling, for example, he decided to let a third person enter into the intimacies of his marital relationship and let it affect his view of himself. He was again allowing the influence of someone else, yet doing so with an act of will that precluded any loss of free will in his life.

The biblical story of Job gives an example of the importance of relationships in developing a self-image. Job had lost possessions, family, wealth, and, finally, health. Yet his friends not only did not help him much at times but they also were threatening to his sense of worth. (Here was a man buffeted by Satan—at the outset of the book of Job we are told that Job's sufferings arose from a challenge of Satan to God. Today, when we increasingly see the influence of the occult in our culture, the reality of Satan at war with God should not be hard to believe.) Yet Job was courageous enough to say, "Though he [God] slay me yet will I trust him." Still his friends chipped away at him, questioning why he was suffering, implying that great sin had caused a severe punishment from God. In my opinion, there are few more severe tests than to suffer and then to have someone put you down for that suffering. Yet that is just what Job's friends did.

In essence, they were saying, "What's wrong with you, Job? How have you sinned? Confess your sins and you'll be blessed and happy again!" How simple: If you hurt, you're sinning; if you're happy, you're righteous. How totally opposed to the teachings of the greatest preacher of the nineteenth century, Charles Spurgeon, when he said, "Men will never become great in divinity until they become great in suffering." And what a put-down to say that when you hurt you have sinned. Yet in the end God took the pain away from Job and restored his life to him in all its fullness when Job prayed for his friends. God did not approve of Job's friend's behavior, but he did require love and forgiveness on Job's part.

In contrast to Job's experience with his friends, the Bible teaches a positive truth about relationships; the body of Christ (the Christian community) is to build up its various members, to increase their level of good self-esteem. I Corinthians 12 reads

> Our bodies have many parts but the many parts make up only one body when they are all put together. So it is with the "body" of Christ. . . . But the Holy Spirit has fitted us all

together into one body. Yes, the body has many parts, not just one part. If the foot says, "I am not a part of the body because I am not a hand," that does not make it any less a part of the body. . . . He has made many parts for our bodies and has put each part just where He wants it. What a strange thing a body would be if it had only one part. So he has made many parts, but still there is only one body. The eye can never say to the hand, "I don't need you." And some of the parts that seem weakest and least important are really the most necessary. . . . If one part suffers, all parts suffer with it, and if one part is honored, all the parts are glad. (TLB)

This passage concludes with a description of the proper functioning of the body in love: "If you love someone you will be loyal to him no matter what the cost. You will always believe in him, always expect the best of him, and always stand your ground in defending him." Given this definition of the interrelatedness of Christians and the clear definition of love, the Christian community has a giant tool at its disposal in elevating the self-esteem of its members. To belong, to be loved, to be needed, to experience loyalty is to feel acceptable and worthwhile.

Functioning supportively in the Christian community, or, indeed, within any group of people, often involves something more than great acts. Endowments that build great cathedrals, donations that feed the masses, campaigns that preach to thousands about the love of God all have their place. But a simple lunch with someone who needs to talk, a supportive note to one who has been unjustly criticized—these acts communicate worth to a person.

I have some friends who live out of town. When I visit, they quietly buy food that I can eat comfortably, since I'm moderately allergic to certain foods. Their concern, as well as the fact that they don't make a big deal out of it, makes me feel loved and good about myself. I know they prefer wheat bread over rye. Yet there they are, eating rye krisp as though they did it every day and preferred it.

Once I called a little girl, a former patient, about a year after I had seen her. It had been a tough case, and I hoped she was still OK. She was. But her spontaneous response to my phone call was, "Gee, you mean you called *just* to see how I was? That's neat!" Just a phone call ... but it helped reinforce a child's good view of herself.

In the same way, people's self-images can be dented and bruised by small things in a relationship. To some, a tone of voice, a disgusted look, or an attitude of indifference can mean the difference between a temporary sense of well-being and feelings of worthlessness. Amy Carmichael says, "Some are wonderfully created. They can go through a thick flight of stinging arrows and hardly feel them. It is as if they were clad in fine chain-armor. Others are made differently. The arrows pierce, and most sharply if they be shot by friends. The very tone of a voice can depress such a one for a week. (It can uplift, too; for the heart that is open to hurt is also very open to love.)"[1]

Often one can observe this most clearly in small children. One little girl who had just lost her mother sat drawing in my playroom. I watched her intently for a while. Then I looked away, and my thoughts wandered as

I looked out at the street. Suddenly Laura crumbled up the drawing and threw it on the floor. Tears filled her eyes, and she exclaimed, "I'm no good. I can't even draw!" For a moment, I had become absorbed in my own thoughts, and she interpreted it as boredom with her, that she was no good.

On an adult level, we too often walk away from new people, unaware of their feelings of aloneness. Yet we are the first to scream if someone treats us with indifference in a place where we are the strangers. We forget to smile at that person who may be afraid to smile first for fear of rejection. We often totally ignore children because "they don't understand anyway." We shout at waiters in restaurants and frown at people we don't even know. And, on the freeway, we forget anyone's feelings! When some people get behind a wheel, they ignore the feelings of all other human beings. Yet once in a while an unusual human being stops in the middle of a traffic jam to let us through, and we feel better about ourselves because of that small but positive encounter.

If trivia are important in making us feel good or bad about ourselves, we should actively choose the input that will make us feel better. When I'm down, I choose *not* to be around negative people. They're hard enough to take when I feel up! Taking my dog for a walk near the school playground that is near my apartment usually involves me in delightful contacts with children. Besides, my dog always responds positively to me. After heavy mental concentration on my work, I like to shop in a grocery store where I usually meet friendly people scattered in among the rest. Dinner with a good friend or a telephone conversation can be uplifting for both people involved. An encounter between two people who respect each other has a way of making both feel better even without any direct communication of those feelings. None of these examples involve deep relationships, but such small incidents make up a bulk of our lives and can be controlled more by us than we sometimes believe.

However, as much as relationships influence our view of ourselves we must ultimately go beyond them in the consideration of developing good self-images. For the adult, relationships alone should not be the sole basis of a person's self-image. Relationships with people should build on an inner core of independent self-trust; they should depend on what we and God already think about our worth. Suppose a friend denigrates us? We should be self-confident enough to turn that put-down off if it is inaccurate.

Psychiatrist Rollo May states this aspect well in his book *Man's Search for Himself*:

> Every human being gets much of his sense of his own reality out of what others say to him and think about him. But many modern people have gone so far in their feeling of reality that they are afraid that without it they would lose the sense of their own existence. They feel they would be "dispersed," like water flowing every which way on the sand. Many people are like blind men feeling their way along in life only by means of touching a succession of there people. ... Social acceptance, "being liked," has so much power because it holds the feelings of loneliness at bay. A person is

surrounded with comfortable warmth; he is merged in the group. He is reabsorbed—as though, in the extreme psychoanalysis symbol, he were to go back into the womb. He temporarily loses his loneliness; but it is at the price of giving up his existence as an identity in his own right. And he renounces the one thing which would get him constructively over the loneliness in the long run, namely the developing of his own inner resources, strength and sense of direction; and using this as a basis for meaningful relations with others.[2]

Those who function effectively in the Body of Christ fulfill two psychological and spiritual requirements for a good self-image. First of all *who* they are is someone they can respect, both from *how* they minister in the body of Christ and in what way they are ministered *to*. I approached a lady in the neighborhood whose husband had just had a stroke and offered some concrete help. She responded almost incredulously hardly believing that I could really care, and I felt good about me and who I was. I sat up with a young girl who wanted to take her life and tried to make her desire life again. Once more I felt good about me. Conversely, when my friend took an hour out of an impossible day to have lunch with me after a personal crisis, I felt worthwhile because of her love. In my office, I hear of people who reach out and cook for people who are sick, listen to people who are lonely, rejoice in another person's success. A minister takes three hours out of his only night at home, to talk to a teenage girl. A doctor visits a patient at 11:30 P.M. because he "*might* need medical assistance before morning." He could have sent him to the emergency room of the local hospital. In turn, these people too are ministered unto. These people who operate in the two-sided ministry of the body of Christ can like who they are before God and humanity.

Additionally, functioning within the body of Christ brings with it a sense of meaning and purpose in life. Viktor Frankl's often quoted, "He who knows a 'why for living will surmount almost every how,' "[3] summarizes this aspect of a good self-image. Because we live in an identity-oriented culture, we do not properly emphasize the part of us that revolves around *where* we are going. Frankl says, concerning two people contemplating suicide, "Both used a phrase which was a stereotype in the camp: 'I have nothing more to expect of life.' Now, the vital requirement was to have the two undergo a Copernican reversal such that they should no longer ask *what they could expect from life*, but were made aware of the fact that *life was awaiting something from them*—that for each of them, indeed for all, somebody or something was waiting, whether it was a piece of work to be done or another human being."[4]

Nor does Frankl view anyone as being beyond the point where his or her fragmented life can come together and have purpose. A remarkable case study concerns a Dr. J., known at one time as "the mass murderer of Steinhof," which was a large mental hospital in Vienna.

> When the Nazis had started their euthanasia program, he held all the strings in his hands and was so fanatic in the job assigned to him that he tried not to let one single psychotic

individual escape the gas chamber. When I came back to Vienna—after having myself escaped from being sent to the gas chamber in Auschwitz—I asked what had happened to Dr. J. "He had been imprisoned by the Russians in one of the isolation cells of Steinhof," they told me. "The next day, however, the door of his cell stood open and Dr. J. was never seen again." Later I was convinced that, like others, he had, by the help of his comrades, found his way to South America. More recently, however, I was consulted by a former high-ranking Austrian diplomat who had been imprisoned behind the Iron Curtain for many years, first in Siberia, and then in the famous Ljubljanka prison in Moscow. While I was examining him neurologically, he suddenly asked me whether I happened to know Dr. J. After my affirmative reply, he continued, "I made his acquaintance in Ljubljanka then he died at about forty, from cancer of the urinary bladder. Before he died, however, he showed himself to be the best comrade you can imagine! He gave consolation to everybody. He lived up to the highest conceivable moral standard. He was the best friend I ever met during my long years in prison!"

This is the story of Dr. J., "the mass murderer of Steinhof." How can you dare to predict the behavior of man!"[5]

Perhaps Frankl's attitude toward human potential for change is one of the most important factors in the development of a positive self-image through relationships. A common question in my counseling relationships is, "Can I make it and can I really become different—can I change and be comfortable with myself?" Too often these people have come from families where they were told "You'll never make it" or, more subtly, "Why can't you be like your older brother or sister!" We all need to be believed in. We need to know we can change and grow. We need to hear that we're OK.

In my experience as a schoolteacher, the general tendency to pigeonhole students deeply troubled me. Johnny was going to fail English because his brother Kent had failed; Susie was going to be a classroom behavior problem because her record said that she had been "hyperactive" in third grade. People seem to be unwilling to let people change. We are reluctant to believe that people can grow, can make it. And we too feel people doubting us when we are insecure about ourselves. The world is crying out for someone who believes in people's ability to grow. And Christians, who have the power of Christ to facilitate that change, ought to be most optimistic, rather than gloomy.

When in a relationship we feel that other people believe in us, we begin to feel more confident about ourselves. I have certain friends who are very strong in their feelings about my capabilities, and I feel the same about them. When one of us is down, the other can be a positive reinforcer that brings the depressed one up again.

My health is not particularly good at times, and there are moments when I feel rather sensitive on this point, especially when it inconveniences others or cuts back on something I really want to do. A few months ago, I went with two friends to a rather remote little village in Mexico. I was a little nervous about the idea of getting sick, both because I was unsure of any available medical facility and also because I didn't want to be a drag to my friends. Even before I left, both friends spoke and acted as though they were not only sure I would be OK, but if I got sick no one would be upset and I would be able to get whatever help I needed. They didn't expect me to get sick, but they were accepting about it if I did. By the time I left, I hardly thought about becoming ill. I thoroughly enjoyed the ten days I was gone and was reasonably strong physically. Actually, I did spend one day in bed. But that day I felt deep empathy from my friends; they understood. Neither of them hovered over me with the kind of anxiety that only makes you feel worse.

Because of a good relationship with two friends, my sensitive spot (getting sick) did not make me feel inadequate. Partly because of their positive attitude, I felt I handled the one day of illness well, and I didn't waste time worrying about getting sick. Because I handled myself well, I felt good about my worth.

Maybe the essence of a good self-image as it relates to friends was shown to me in that trip to Mexico. I knew we would be living closely together for ten days, and whatever weaknesses and strengths we had would be tested. I learned to do what is hard for me: to be sick, accept it, and still like myself. In a sense, I learned to respect myself more for how well I coped rather than to put myself down for being ill. Two good relationships helped me do that.

In concluding the foreword to my book *To Anger, With Love*, Paul Tournier wrote, "We all stand in need of a great deal of love in order to be able to accept ourselves as we really are."[6] That statement perhaps summarizes it all. Those who have the best self-image are people who have faced who they are and why they are here. They then have grown and changed within that framework. To do that effectively, we need the support of good relationships with responsible people.

NOTES

1. Amy Carmichael, *Kohila: The Shaping of an Indian Nurse* (Pennsylvania: Christian Literature Crusade, undated), p. 129.
2. Rollo May, *Man's Search for Himself* (New York: Norton, 1953), pp. 32–33.
3. Viktor E. Frankl, *Psychotherapy and Existentialism* (New York: Simon & Schuster, 1967), p. 103.
4. Frankl (1967), p. 104.
5. Frankl (1967), p. 62.
6. Elizabeth R. Skoglund, *To Anger, With Love* (New York: Harper & Row, 1977), p. 11.

CHAPTER 3

I Am What I Do

Even during his first session, Mark was unusually self-aware. When he walked into my office, he said, "My marriage is about to break up, and I feel that a lot of it may be my fault. I'm not sure I even like myself anymore."

As we analyzed his feelings about himself and his expectation in his marriage, several things became obvious. Mark really didn't like himself very much at all. He had been the "lord and master" of his household at the beginning of his marriage and had lost his wife's love. Since then he had changed to the extreme opposite and allowed himself to be walked over. He then lost Joan's respect. He had expressed irrational anger to his children, and so they avoided him. The job Mark faced in therapy was to see a low self-image as his root problem and then to do something to change it. Relationships would help. Talking about his worth would be important. And he had to change his behavior if he was to realistically raise his sense of self-worth.

Mark's first move was to stop allowing his wife to denigrate him. When she told him that she was leaving for the evening and then *ordered* him to watch the children, he firmly told her he had other plans. "In the future," he explained, "please let me know earlier when you want me to babysit and let's schedule our times away so they don't conflict." Surprised by her husband's attitude, Joan complied.

Two days later, Joan was depressed about the death of a close friend. Mark sent her roses. He had never been tender before, and again Joan was surprised.

At first Mark had been brutal and inconsiderate. Then he had become a weak man who could command no one's respect. Now he was altering his behavior once more, this time to a man strong enough to be gentle and sure enough of himself to command respect. Now he was really changing on a gut level. He could assert his rights without rage. He could feel tender without having his masculinity threatened. And each time he did something that reflected this new self-image that self-image grew still stronger.

Tricia was seven. Already children in the neighborhood avoided her. When she was angry, she would trip them or hit them and then declare innocently, "It was just an accident." Yet these "accidents" happened with alarming regularity. Teachers wanted her transferred out of their classes, and parents of classmates forbade her to visit their homes. She was a lonely little girl. One day she blurted out a very adult statement: "I don't like myself." When I asked her why, she responded, "Because no one likes me. I have no friends. Nobody ever wants to play with me."

After a few discussions on why people might not like her—her bossiness, her insistence on her own way, her physical attacks on people and objects when she became angry—she quite suddenly seemed happy. When I asked her what had happened, her answer was once again amazingly adult: "I decided to change because I want people to like me."

Most seven-year-olds, or those older, do not change as fast as this child. Because Tricia could face her behavior and its consequences and then alter her actions accordingly, she changed into a person she could respect and whom others respected, too. An alteration of behavior affected her level of self-esteem.

Yet change involves effort and time, and we are a people who are used to quick, easy answers. We have pills to make us happy, to calm us down, to pep us up. The younger generation loses itself in a cloud of sweet-smelling smoke while the older generation, as well as the younger, obliterates its feelings of pain with cocktails. We speculate to gain fast money, and we expect psychotherapists to wave away our problems with a facile move of their magic wands. Yet we are empty, incredibly empty. And we wonder why we live and who we really are.

We who are Christians are no less simplistic in our approach. We want to experience the love of God in our lives and wonder why he seems so distant. Yet, in our guilt over our inability to keep up with our self-imposed demands, we put God at a distance. We project our self-rejection on him and feel that he too is displeased with us. Again we have sought for easy answers and failed. We too often have judged ourselves and other Christians by how many times a week we attend church, by attendance at theaters and dances, by whether or not we drink alcohol, while our lives are riddled with deep inconsistencies of deceit and lack of love. It is easier to turn down a glass of wine than it is to love the unloveable. It is easier to sign a college pledge promising not to attend the theater than to earn grades without cheating or to keep the confidence of a friend.

We have taken the easy way of legalism rather than remembering that "Commandments are walls around the playground." They are guidelines, not always absolutes; principles, not always specifics. According to Paul Tournier "moralism, the religion of good works, gradually reentered the heart of Protestantism" following the Reformation. Tournier continues,

> It is significant that a Protestant patient of mine could say to me, "Protestantism seems to me to be an immense effort to earn grace by good conduct, whilst Catholicism freely dispenses this grace to any who seek it from a priest." The patient was not wrong. Moralism has reestablished the idea of merit of a grace which is conditional. And in some Protestant circles these conditions so proliferate and harden down as to be oppressive. I know a young lady the authorities of whose church disapproved because she had spoken to

a woman wearing a red jumper; such clothing was regarded as a sign of frivolity and it was blameworthy to have anything to do with so worldly a person.[1]

It is in deeper behavioral changes that one's relationship with God and one's own self-image are built. We must *have* worth to *feel* worth.

A brief incident pointed out to me how little trust people have in other people. A man on a plane turned to me and said, "Maybe a divine providence brought us together for this limited time. I need to talk, but I'm afraid to trust. But I'll never see you again, so it's safe!"

"I'll never see you again, so it's safe!" Many people feel this way, because so many cannot be trusted. To be trusted is to have established a behavior pattern that is tremendously ego building. If people trust me, I feel a sense of worth. To be trustworthy requires growth, ethics, self-control. It develops. It is not easy, and so relatively few people achieve this goal. Honesty, hard work, worship of God, compassion toward others—all these are hard-won qualities. But they make up the person who can look at him- or herself and say, "I am comfortable with this person who I am."

Growth in self-esteem that is achieved by change in behavioral patterns is difficult, for we are all a little resistant to change. Change threatens us; it means we will be different. It annoys us because it requires action and work. I am convinced that flexibility to change is the great yardstick of age. Some people can always change and they are forever young. Others are old at fifteen because what they are and have is all they ever want.

Change and one's attitude toward it is the pivotal point of the success or failure of psychotherapy. Perhaps that is one reason why some fear therapy. To enter therapy is to put oneself in a position of willingness to change.

To each of us, change in another human being seems easy. Why can't the irascible be kind, the alcoholic stop drinking, the untruthful become honest? Why can't the *other* person change? Yet when that person who must change becomes *me*, we realize the difficulties involved.

Perhaps the first and most painful step in change is facing the specific need in oneself. Years ago when I was a high school teacher, I faced this problem. I started my career teaching biology and English, well trained and effective. I expected perfect attention from my students and serious work both in the classroom and without. My students sat in straight rows, in alphabetical order, and they were to speak one at a time when called on. In theory, it sounded just right. But with today's youth it didn't work. Doggedly I plodded on. Facing me at the end of a day were long lists of names of those who had broken some rule and were required to stay after school. But there were two problems: I had to stay after school, too, and behavior did not improve. It was me against them, a power struggle that relegated the study of Byron, Shelley, and Keats to a definite second place in priorities.

Then my moment of awareness came: I was too rigid. I was failing as a teacher, not because I couldn't teach but because I had alienated my students with all my rigid rules. There is a parallel in the Christian life where we make the rules so all-important that people see the negative aspects of Christianity rather than the person of Jesus Christ in all his love and perfection.

Facing that I was rigid, that I had to change to be the kind of teacher I really wanted to be, was difficult. But it was the first, necessary step toward becoming a really good teacher and liking myself for that. Then came a process of trial and error in which I gradually achieved a balanced position. I forced myself toward flexibility by avoiding such patterns as alphabetical seating. I chatted more informally with my students between classes. Above all, I changed. I decided that what they learned was important, not where they sat. I tried to share my interest in literature with them, not just the facts. And my reward was watching them really grow to love certain aspects of literature. The teacher I was to begin with did not do much for my feelings of self-worth. The teacher I became made me feel good about myself.

It is difficult for my patients to face unpleasant aspects of themselves. Recently I had to help confront a little girl with the fact that people rejected her because she hurt them and cared only about her own rights. I helped a woman face the fact that she couldn't continue to cheat on her husband and like herself. A young man faced the realization that smoking weed was destroying his motivation. The little girl left with the remark, "I better come back next week because I might have a problem by then." She's only six. She didn't want to admit that she was wrong in hurting people. But once it was talked through she wanted to change. For all of them, facing the *need* for change was painful, but they felt a sense of relief that at last they had confronted *themselves* at their worst point and they could now grow and change. In the very act of being courageous enough to face themselves they raised their level of self-esteem.

It is one thing to see the need for change and another to put the need into action. By the time the six-year-old had reached home, she had already hit her brother. The housewife wanted to go out with her secret lover that weekend, and the young man who smoked marijuana found that his friends were rough on him when he refused to smoke with them.

Perhaps herein lies one of the great strengths of Christianity. Those without Christ often *want* to change and find that they lack the power to effect that change. One of the great teachings of Jesus Christ is that people can be changed. Christianity does not just offer a passport to Heaven. It offers the possibility of change. Amy Carmichael gives a graphic illustration of God's ability to change even dispositions, that most intimate part of our being. Amy Carmichael was a missionary in South India during the first half of this century. A deeply sensitive and intelligent woman, she dedicated her life to the saving of children sold to the gods in the temples of southern India.

Speaking of one of these children, Carmichael says,

> She was barely ten, but for what seemed to her a long time she had been asking questions which no one could answer, not even her wise old father to whom she had shyly brought them.
>
> There was something austere about the child, something

that, in the mood which was upon her then, would have made one who saw her think of a little grey rock cropping up among greenery. But there was something wistful too. She was wrapped in a sari, bright like a blackberry leaf in September, or the breast of a forest minivet, the one warm note of color there, and she waited, still as a leaf, for something to happen, for someone to speak.

"Who of all the gods was the God of gods, the Sovereign God, Creator?" That had been the first question she had brought to her father. Was it the heavenly Siva, whose ashes she rubbed on her forehead every morning after bathing? There were so many gods, she grew puzzled as she counted them all. Was it Siva? Could he change dispositions? If only she could find this out she would be satisfied, for the god who could change dispositions must be the greatest, and surely the greatest must be the Creator. . . . There was one way, she reflected, by which she could bring creatorship and sovereignty down to the test of practical life. She would go through all the gods she knew and find out which of them could change dispositions. . . .

For she had a hot temper. Often when she was playing with other children something would provoke her and she would break out in anger, whereupon they would run away and refuse to play with her. She had tried to conquer the fault but there it was, strong and growing stronger in her. She prayed to Siva. . . . "Change my disposition so that other children may love me and wish to play with me. . . ."

But her disposition had not been changed. She had appealed to several other gods, but nothing had happened. She was all alone now—with whom?

She waited awhile in silence, the unanswering green things about her, the empty blue sky above her and cried, "O God, God of all the gods, hear me!"[2]

Then she went home—home to a baby brother whom she had nursed from the first hour of his life. Then he died, at nine months of age, of a dysentery. And the little sister felt desolate as they carried his body away. Again she had questions: Would he be lonely? Who would care for him now? Now she wondered if this Creator whom she had sought could be good. How could He take this little brother? How could he disappoint a little girl? And still on she searched.

Some days later she went to draw water as usual and saw a crowd. Then she heard the words, *"There is a living God. There is a living God: He turned me, a lion, into a lamb."*[3] She heard and came back and heard more. She tested in her own ways to see if this could truly be the living God, the Creator, who could change dispositions.

> She knew now who could change dispositions, and that He, the living God, had appeared to her in the tent as the loving God too. This had sweetened all her thought about her little brother, though she still longed to know for certain where he had gone.... She had never heard proper prayer ... and so she spoke as a child would, just as she felt: "I cannot live so long without knowing more of You."[4]

After stating her needs, she boldly concluded, "If You who created me cannot do this for me, who can?"[5] Then at last she met those who taught her more of the God who could change dispositions, although there was much conflict with family and much grief. There were frequent delays and great suffering. But perhaps it is not too simple to relegate the symbolism of the mystic Francis Thompson in his poem "The Hound of Heaven" to the experience of this child. Thompson speaks of the pursuit of God after man. These same words summarize to me the spiritual journey of the child in southern India:

> Ah, fondest, blindest, weakest,
> I am He whom thou seekest!
> Thou drawest love from thee, who drawest Me.[6]

Perhaps the greatness of the meeting between this child and God lies in the human improbability of such a meeting. A child? Alone? In India? But God was seeking her and that made all the difference.

But how interesting that in such a pagan atmosphere this child would decide that God would be God if he could change dispositions! Not if he removed mountains or consumed enemies with fire but if he would curb a bad temper. So we, too, know the God who changes us—with one requirement: our commitment and our faith.

F. B. Meyer, a well-known nineteenth-century preacher, shares his experience with this God who changes us:

> Years before, when engaged in a gathering of unruly and noisy children, he had been suddenly driven to claim from the Savior the gift of His own gentle patience, in the words, "Thy patience, Lord!" And instantly so divine a calm filled his spirit that he realized that he had made a great discovery. And from that moment he had retained the extremes of his brief petition, inserting between them the grace, the lack of which was hurrying him to sin. In moments of weakness, "Thy strength, Lord!" or in moments of conscious strength, "Thy humility, Lord!" When assailed by unholy suggestions, "Thy purity, Lord!" or when passing through deep waters of trial, "Thy resignation and restfulness, Lord!"[7]

Meyer, too, like the Indian child, had found the God who changes dispositions. And there is a universality of that experience. For in a personal relationship with God, men since the beginning of time and in all age groups and in every social strata have also found in God a potential for change. A chance to be someone likeable, someone worth knowing.

For the Christian, when all the determination in the world seems futile, there is the God who *can* change dispositions, a fact that is summarized by hymn writer A. B. Simpson in the refrain, "I Take, He Undertakes." He does the changing, I do the taking. The glorious fact of Christianity is that when we reach the end of our self-reform there is God who can change us or help us change.

In addition to God who changes us, our own human will comes into sharp focus. Unlike some who teach that we are total victims of our environment and genes, I believe by sheer guts we *can* change much in our lives. Anger sometimes helps. Anger against a physical disability, for example, can motivate a person to change and achieve more than he or she would have without the disability. A friend of mine who was deeply distressed decided one day that her depression would no longer control her. And it didn't.

Beyond change, however, there is one other aspect of self-worth, as it relates to behavior, that requires consideration: the self-acknowledgment of change. A young lady in her twenties made considerable progress in the development of responsible attitudes and behavior. In short, she had changed from a woman who cared little about the rights of others to a person who helped many people and did her job at work with care and precision. From a person who came to work late and shoved off her own duties in typing and filing to a girl who worked under her, she became someone who helped the other at her job when the workload became excessively heavy for them. She felt better about herself as a result, but the full impact of how much she had changed did not fully hit until I pointed it out to her. She had changed, but in order for that change to raise her self-image she had to see it and recognize it.

We mistake humility for low self-esteem and tend to admire self-abnegation. Actually, God wants us to see ourselves as we are and give ourselves credit for what is worthwhile and what has been achieved through change, credit from both ourselves and others. Change unacknowledged does not elevate one's self-image.

Jason was fifteen when he first came to me with a drug problem. His parents, who were very strict, legalistic Christians, wanted him home at excessively early hours on weekends and in general made rules that made him stand out as different from even the Christian boys he knew. Jason rebelled, took more drugs, and broke every rule he could. Finally after months of counseling he tapered off and, for the sake of his own self-image, began to live more responsibly. He kept reasonable hours, which by now his parents had conceded to, and stopped using drugs. His self-image started to improve, but his parents refused to give him any credit for his positive change. Instead, the better he behaved, the stricter their rules became, until once again what they expected of him was so impossible that he could not live up to those expectations.

Thoroughly discouraged, Jason saw me for a last session. "I won't come back," he stated. "It just won't help. The more I improve, the harder life gets at home. I might as well give up and do what I want." And give up he did because neither he nor those he loved recognized his progress sufficiently and gave credit for all the change he had made.

Change improves one's self-image—but only if that change is recognized as worthy. The human personality is sturdy enough to endure the atrocities of a Dachau and Auschwitz and yet fragile enough to need the acceptance of itself and others in knowing that it truly is OK. To know we're OK requires a combination of self-awareness and the approval of others, which combine to make us know that how we behave makes us worthwhile human beings.

NOTES

1. Paul Tournier, *Guilt and Grace* (New York: Harper & Row, 1962).
2. Amy Carmichael, *Ploughed Under* (London: S•P•C•K, 1953), pp. 13–16.
3. Carmichael (1953), p. 26.
4. Carmichael (1953), pp. 38–39.
5. Carmichael (1953), p. 39.
6. *Poetry of the Victorian Period* Woods & Buckley, (New York: Scott, Foresman & Company, 1930; 1955) *The Hound of Heaven*, Francis Thompson (p. 848).
7. F. B. Meyer, *Christian Living* (New York: Revell, 1892), pp. 13–14.

CHAPTER 4

God Says I'm OK

There I was. Right in the middle. A close friend had adopted a baby boy through me from one of my patients. The child had been taken home directly from the hospital by his adoptive parents. They loved him deeply, and now at five and one-half months, just before the final signing of the adoption papers, he was cute, alert, and the joy of their lives.

The first six months of adoption is always a nervous time, for at any point the real mother can change her mind. But by now the Barretts were confident. After all, the signing of the papers was only two weeks away.

At the same time, the baby's real mother, Joyce, had continued in therapy with me and had grown greatly in her emotional strength. She had developed some healthy friendships with people who helped her like herself, instead of the usual group of losers with whom she had been previously aligned. She had redeveloped her skills as a typist and was working full time. And for the very first time in her life she was dating a young man who really cared about her and their relationship. This was unusual for a woman who had known little of tenderness from any man, including her father.

Now came the dilemma. Adoption had been successful: the right parents for the right baby. They even looked alike. Therapy had been effective: A young, unwed mother had established the beginning of a new life for herself. But this now-stronger young lady wanted her baby back. My success as a therapist was about to boomerang and make me feel like a failure. If the mother had stayed weak, she would have left the baby with its adoptive parents, but I would not have done a good job. But would my expertise as a therapist hurt an innocent baby and its already vulnerable new parents? I had the sinking feeling that nothing I could have done would have felt right, except to have totally ignored the case and to have referred it to someone else. Even that would have felt like failure.

But, as I focused on God's view of me, the feelings of failure left. My self-image became positive once again. I had taken the case under his direction and had been successful as a therapist with all the people involved. The decisions they now made were their own responsibility, not mine. And I could rest in the knowledge that before God I had done right, and therefore I could like myself. In speaking of the value one should put on such incidents of life, Amy Carmichael aptly comments,

> *For the eternal substance of a thing never lies in the thing itself, but in the quality of our reaction toward it.* If in hard times we are kept from resentment, held in silence and filled with inward sweetness, that is what matters. The event that distressed us will pass from memory as a wind that passes and is gone. But what we were while the wind was blowing upon us has eternal consequences.[1]

And "what we were" should have a profound effect on how we view ourselves.

Unfortunately, too often in evangelical circles God is viewed as primarily punitive and judgmental. We indeed project our feelings of self-rejection on him as though he were the source. Once, when I felt particularly down, I commented to a friend, "I feel like my relationship with God is shattered." Then, as I thought about these words, I realized that God had not changed and I had not sinned. But my self-image was down, and so I imagined that God, too, was not happy with me.

Christians often tend to cultivate this negative view of God. Preachers in the pulpit exhort their hearers to "Confess their depression" or to "Renounce themselves." Now renouncing yourself, in the biblical context, means to commit the totality of your life and goods to Christ. But that is not what the average churchgoer perceives in that commandment. One even wonders if that is what the average pastor means when he says it. Rather, a form of self-hate is implied. God does not view worth the way we do. First of all, he *starts* on a positive note, with "You *have* worth." Then he goes on to say, "I will give you *more* worth."

The other day, I told a woman that she was not the primary cause of her child's problems. She became even more upset and said, "I know I caused Susan to be emotionally disturbed because I've never been a good mother." Her feelings of guilt were already so deep that she actually wanted those feelings reinforced. For me to think that she was OK when she was convinced she was not OK only made her feel greater guilt. Someday, perhaps, she will be able to have the courage to honestly look at herself, and she will be pleasantly surprised to find that she has worth.

Our distorted idea of the "good Christian" is of one who is always nice, frequently walked over, and certainly never angry. Yet that is a definition of the very opposite kind of person from the one who accomplishes his or her God-given task in this world. To be self-preserving, to guard one's energies and rights, to survive—this is right because it then enables a person to do those things in this world that are really important.

This concept is different from the usual idea of selfishness. Selfishness grasps for itself, wants to be indulged. To be preserving of self is to have priorities in one's life that preserve life for its primary task. Christ did that at the age of twelve in the temple, where, after leaving his parents while they searched for hours for him, he merely said that he must be about his father's business. Selfish? No. Self-preserving? Yes, even from the demands of godly parents. Again, Christ acted with the same sense of priorities when he left the crowds with all of their needs in order to rest.

God puts a higher value on human worth than we ever could, and his judgments are at times less hard than ours.

As I rode along a road in the interior of Mexico, I kept seeing crosses—just one single cross at a time—at various, unpredictable spots on the road. They marked, I was told, the grave of a person who had died on that spot. I suppose in the tropical heat there was often little else to do but immediately bury someone. The area was remote, and even though I stayed in that 150-mile radius for over a week I never saw a church. Yet every grave had a cross. Intuitively, these people clung to the cross as a sign of hope, as a symbol of their eternal worth, as something positive even in death. Perhaps we should view God more simply, as these people did.

John 9:1–3 describes Christ as he walks along a road and sees a man blind from birth. "Master," his disciples asked him, "Why was this man born blind? Was it a result of his own sins or those of his parents?" It never entered their minds to regard this man in his imperfection in any light but that of sin. Here a man's worth was judged by his physical infirmity.

The view that if you're ill, depressed, afraid, belong to the "wrong" race, or are in general below par makes you a less worthwhile human being is not a Christian teaching. Christ's answer to whether or not the man's blindness came from sin was a definite no. Rather, he put a positive construction on the situation and said that the infirmity was "to demonstrate the power of God." Then he healed him. With his infirmity, the blind man had worth. And Jesus Christ, once that point was established, went on to give him an even greater range of ability in which to serve.

How many a great saint prostrated helplessly on a bed of suffering has prayed for an active evangelist who might not have had so active a ministry without his or her prayers. Much worship of God has come out of the suffering of bereavement and loss. I think of Hudson Taylor in the interior of China—alone, having just lost his young wife and baby—softly singing, "Jesus, I am resting, resting in the joy of what Thou art. I am finding out the greatness of Thy loving heart." Yet he too had his down moments. But great trust and worship to God arose out of such moments of anguish.

But even if a person's worth is not diminished by human frailty, a lack of comprehension of that worth can become a real problem. People suffering from the rejection of a divorce, the loss of a job, accumulated personal losses, or failure in a life goal cannot help but feel the effects in how they view themselves. They still *have* worth, and, depending on how they handle their problems, perhaps that worth is even greater than before. But they do not *feel* their worth. And so the symptoms begin: ulcers, migraine headaches, anxiety attacks, sexual insecurity, depression, anger, and a myriad of other manifestations. I am encountering numerous professional people who cannot find jobs that in any way reflect or relate to their training. People with Ph.D.'s are sweeping floors in grocery stores; teachers are brushing up on their none-too-good typing skills. One young former female executive said to me, "I can't even find volunteer work that suits my training." The result in this young woman was a gut desire each morning to never wake up and face another day. In each person, the problem becomes how to once again like oneself. Or, if for a variety of reasons one has never liked oneself, how for the first time can one begin to like oneself? One way is through a relationship with God that involves a deep, gut-level commitment.

C. S. Lewis makes some helpful comments on commitment. It does not mean that you must meet all the demands made on the natural self:

> The Christian way is different: harder and easier. Christ says, "Give Me all. I don't want so much of your time and so much of your money and so much of your work: I want you. I have not come to torment your natural self, but to kill it. No half measures are any good. I don't want to cut off a branch here and a branch there, I want to have the whole tree down. I don't want to drill the tooth, or crown it, or stop it, but to have it out. Hand over the whole natural self, all the desires which you think innocent as well as the ones you think wicked—the whole outfit. I will give you a new outfit instead. In fact, I will give you Myself: my own will shall become yours."[2]

Then added Lewis, wisely,

> We can only do it for moments at first. But from those moments the new sort of life will be spreading through our system: because now we are letting Him work at the right part of us. It is the difference between paint, which is merely laid on the surface, and a dye or stain, which soaks right through. He never talked vague, idealistic gas. When He

said "Be perfect," He meant it. He meant we must go in for the full treatment.[3]

"The full treatment" means that I let go of my entire being to the total ownership and daily control of God. He owns *me*, not just the works I do, for they are merely by-products of who I am. It is then that the deepest sense of worth can be felt. If I am becoming all that God wants me to be, I have a rational basis for accepting my own worth.

At times, we can *see* that acceptance by God means we have worth, but we do not *feel* that worth. At such times, it is good to continually remind ourselves of what we know to be true. If we tell ourselves this truth, we will eventually feel the sense of worth that is ours. In that way, intellectually grasped knowledge becomes part of what we experience in the deepest levels of our awareness.

In my own life, commitment has provided relief from tension as well as a sense of increased self-worth. After some accumulated losses, I felt depleted at best and somewhat inadequate at worst. Missing those who had died, I felt an emptiness. Feeling distant from one with whom I had disagreed, I felt inadequacy. Was I really correct? Maybe *I* was wrong. One key to renewal emotionally was to come to God with "Here I am, Lord—confused—fairly sure I'm right but ready to be shown if I'm wrong. Please totally take over my being and fill me with your Spirit." For one brief instant, there was fear. What if God took what I wanted to keep? After all, when God owns you he can do as he likes. Then came the image of the kind father who is offered a favorite toy from his small child. Does he destroy the toy, crush it, just because it has been offered to him and he has the power to ruin it? No, not unless the toy were dangerous or poisonous. Fatherly love would only be made greater by such relinquishment. And is not my heavenly father more loving than any earthly father? Will he give me a stone when I ask for bread? And so my commitment issued forth into a sense of God's presence and *approval,* and I began to feel better about myself.

As a finite human being, however, I have discovered that the *how* of living constantly under God's approval is closely tied in with commitment as a daily act. An act, once done, can be eroded or taken back within hours. It is good if one's first thought on awakening in the morning could be a simple, "I am yours, Lord." In the case of the Christian, at least, it is impossible to have self-love without knowing that one is rightly related to one's God at that very moment. And then, if God says I'm OK, how can I think less?

While many positive feelings of self-worth come from our own reflection on and with God, it would probably be safe to say that most people in the organized church also need people in order for feelings of good self-esteem to be nourished. We don't usually live with God alone.

A young man whose relationship to God has been very close but who suffered from tremendous depression came into my office the other day with the words, "I feel so depressed. The man who led me to Christ told me I shoudn't be coming here. All I need, he feels, is 'in the Word.' " Earlier, too, he had been told that "all he needed was in the Word," until one night he almost called the paramedics. It was then that he started therapy. All he needed *was* in the Word, but not in the sense that his friend had meant it. He needed the emotional support of the body of Christ, not its condemnation—and that's in the Word. He needed medical help—and was not Luke a physician and acceptable as such? He needed counseling—and we read in Proverbs that in a multitude of counselors there is safety. That verse, along with those in Corinthians that refer to gifts of wisdom, discernment, and helps, all imply that some people can counsel better than others. Does a little training make that counseling somehow corrupt?

This man's self-image, which had been nourished by counseling and his personal relationship with God, had been damaged temporarily by his well-meaning but unperceptive friend. He had been made to feel that God no longer approved of him. Thus once again he had to be reassured of God's love and God's acceptance.

I have found, too, that there are various private ways of getting such feelings from God. Yesterday I was too tired to write. Near sundown, I walked down to the beach and wandered among the tidepools. I saw tiny fish darting quickly away from me as I approached. I poked sea urchins, gently, and watched them pull into themselves protectively. And then at the other end of the cove I discovered a sea lover's paradise—a span of beach that during low tide was literally buried in shells. For a long time, I picked, sorted, and collected. My muscles relaxed. I felt tired but stronger. I felt God's peace as I watched the ocean rolling in and out. And I sensed his perfection as I looked at the shells in all of their beauty. I felt permanence in God's plan for my life and the quietness of that beach with its freedom from demands renewed my knowledge that I was OK. Just tired, but quite OK in God's sight. Last night I slept well.

In the nourishment of my own self-image, hymns are often a help. For example, a verse from an old hymn:

> Things which once were wild alarms
> Cannot now disturb my rest;
> Closed in everlasting arms,
> Pillowed on the loving breast.
> Oh, to lie forever here,
> Doubt, and care, and self resign,
> While He whispers in my ear—
> I am His, and He is mine.[4]

Sometimes I just read such words or sing them softly. Once in a while I use a piano. But always they refresh me with the knowledge that God *is* and that to him I am very important. To be important to the God of all creation—how could that lead to anything but an elevated self-image?

There are many moments when the reading of great books reinforces one's feelings of worth. Emerson was correct when he spoke of finding our own rejected thoughts in great writings. When we read that C. S. Lewis and C. H. Spurgeon both panicked over money, we feel better. The fact that Amy Carmichael had poor health for twenty years and used those years to encourage others makes her reader's less likely to put themselves down when they are ill. We may have been accepting in these areas before but to see them on the pages of a book supports us, and once again we feel God's approval in our life.

But, above the ways we know God's approval of us, there is ultimately God's character. God is perfect and complete. Yet he created us in his image *for* his fellowship. Even on earth Christ as God-Man expressed a need for fellowhsip with his disciples. They failed him. Thomas doubted him. Judas betrayed him. Peter, James and John deserted him in Gethsemane. But he was the perfect friend who died for those he loved that they might never die.

In an age when we are once again beginning to see supernatural manifestations of the occult in dramatic ways, we must remember that our God Jehovah, who always was and will be, is stronger than any demonic manifestation. In an age when we also have witnessed the atrocities of Nazi prison camps and other vivid examples of our inhumanity to each other, we are reminded of God's love and tenderness in the middle of our human harshness. I think of God as he walked on this earth and found a crowd ready to stone a woman who had been caught in adultery. Jewish laws permitted stoning, and they were ready to carry out her sentence. With purity, Christ admitted the wrongness of the act. With wisdom and justice, he asked the crowd if they were ever guilty of sin and, if they were not, then to go ahead and throw their stones. Condemned, they dropped their stones and walked away. Christ turned to the woman and with extreme gentleness told her to go and sin no more. No lectures. She knew her sin. No judgment. She had had more than she needed of that and had received forgiveness from the only one present who was without sin.

Here we have a composite of God: all power and wisdom; perfection combined with love and gentleness; love for humanity, yet never allowing that love to become weakening in approving of sin. And this is the God who accepts us and approves of us. How then can we dare to minimize our own worth or anyone else's?

Four-year-old Suzanne came to me a day before her scheduled surgery. Expecting her to be frightened, I entered more cautiously than usual into the counseling session. When I had first met her, Suzanne was a very shy, insecure little girl who didn't like herself at all. Even now she needed much approval. I was surprised, therefore, when she seemed so bright and happy. After a few moments, she smiled at me and said: "I'm fine. My Mommy and Daddy prayed with me last night." Human beings that cared combined with a God who was all-powerful and yet concerned were what this child needed on a bad day to make her feel secure. And what is security but a good, sturdy sense of self-worth?

To be created by God in his image, for his purposes, is a marvelous thing. To feel the sense of worth that should result is sometimes hard, and often requires outside help, but it is valid and real. Perhaps more real than anything else in life.

NOTES

1. Amy Carmichael, *Kohila: The Shaping of an Indian Nurse* (Pennsylvania: Christian Literature Crusade, undated), p. 135.
2. C. S. Lewis, *Mere Christianity* (New York: Macmillan, 1952, 1953, 1961), pp. 163–164.
3. Lewis (1960), p. 165.
4. Wade Robinson, composer, "Loved With Everlasting Love," Paul Beckwith, comp. and ed., in *Hymns*, (Chicago: Inter-Varsity Press, 1952), p. 144.

CHAPTER 5

Growing Beyond Pain

A few days ago, I had a telephone conversation with a four-year-old patient of mine, Jeanette, who, after being molested repeatedly by her father, had been placed in a foster home. For a while, all I heard were sobs. Then, as she was able to talk, I asked, "What's the matter?" "Can I stay here forever," she pleaded, "Or will they take me back home?" I couldn't answer her question because unfortunately I can't control where she lives. The courts will do that. But when I got off the telephone I cried, not for Jeanette alone, but for all the pain this world contains and for our often futile efforts to control it.

For this world does contain much pain, and our attitude toward that pain has a tremendous potential effect on our self-image. Joe came to me in a state of deep depression combined with great anxieties about his sanity and his future success in life. He kept making statements like "Maybe I should be hospitalized" or "There are times when I feel like calling the paramedics." He felt weak because of his depressions and guilty when he had to depend on his wife. Yet each day he went to work, no matter how painful his emotions were, and he still had time to try to cheer up someone else.

During one of our sessions, I pointed out to Joe that while his emotional health was improving and it seemed that someday he would be considerably more comfortable, right now his suffering did not have to be denigrating. On the contrary, his pain could add to his feelings of self-worth if he could change his attitude. Rather than being weak, he was strong when he went to work in spite of his pain. Rather than being self-centered, he was others-centered when he helped people even though he himself hurt. In short, he handled his suffering well, and that should and did make him feel very much better about himself. This attitude directly speeded up his overall recovery because of its positive effect on his self-image.

Similarly, Frankl's theory of logotherapy speaks of "Turning suffering into an achievement, setting an example, thinking of others, providing inspirations."[1] Ultimately, Frankl speaks of suffering in a way that will please one's taskmaster—or God.

In speaking of Frankl's views, Joseph Fabry explains,

> History is full of stories about heroes and martyrs who turned tragedy into triumph. The story is told about Tristan Bernard, the French writer, who, together with his wife, was taken to the Drancy concentration camp by the Nazis. While they were marching in a column of despairing Jews,

Bernard said to his wife, "Up to now we have lived in fear; from now on we will live in hope." From the depths of a situation of despair, he had reversed the entire outlook of the situation, not by changing the situation but by changing his attitude. And his example helped his fellow sufferers to shoulder their lot with courage. Given a cause, even the ordinary man may become a hero. Examples from contemporary history show how the British stood up under the blitz during World War II, and how the Berliners braved the privations during the airlift. They were aware of a meaning behind their suffering, and of the example they set for the rest of the world.

No birth is without labor pains, figuratively and literally. The history of creative people is full of tales of pain, from Michelangelo's "agony and ectasy" to Handel's complete physical exhaustion upon giving birth to his *Messiah*. Frankl speaks of the struggle of the genuine artist who is not satisfied until his hundredth draft of his creation or the tenth version of his work has stood the test of his artistic conscience. It is also questionable whether the moments of bliss in a love relationship could be possible without the "labor pains" of agony and doubt. Yet no true artist would forego his creation, nor the lover his love, because pain is the price. And neither would a mother forego her child because she knows that she will have to endure what is probably the most universal human "suffering" in the world. On the contrary: She is happily suffering pain for the sake of having a child. Imagine, however, her anguish were she to know in advance that her baby was going to be a lifelong mongolian idiot. Yet, when in some unfortunate cases she is faced with the unavoidable fact that her child is an incurable idiot, many a woman will turn this suffering into an achievement by devoting her love to her child, setting an example to other parents in similar tragic circumstances. *It is not the load that breaks us down,* logotherapy seems to say, *but the way we carry it.*[2]

Or, put another way, "suffering can have meaning if it changes *you* (the sufferer) for the better."[3] And when one is changed for the better by how one handles one's pain, suffering elevates that person's self-image.

Pain *cannot* leave a person unchanged. Some react with cynicism and bitterness, some respond with compassion, and a growing number develop a level of despair that leads to suicide or other acts of desperation. What most people fail to realize is that they are not mere pawns of fortune: They *do* have a choice. Perhaps the realization of that fact alone is elevating to one's feelings of self-worth.

Pain can range from discomfort to extreme torture and anguish. Although pain is more commonly thought of as physical, it applies equally to the psychological and the spiritual. The whole person is inter-related. Psychological dreariness may accompany a chronic illness, physical tension often is felt with emotional distress, and spiritual questioning and even numbness can set in when either the body or the mind suffers.

Physical pain is perhaps better understood and accepted than psychological pain. Yet pain is pain, and whether physically based or psychologically created each pain has its heroic potential as well as its own unique hurt. It seems Christian to some people to embrace pain and rejoice in God over it. Praising God for one's difficulties has become very popular. And certainly one should praise God in spite of pain. But it is discouraging to be made to feel that one should praise God *for* pain. Indeed, it seems almost masochistic. Nor is such a teaching to be found in the Scriptures. Christ himself pleaded for deliverance from pain in the Garden of Gethsemane. Another striking example is in the life of King Hezekiah who, when he became deathly ill, pleaded to God for his life and was healed. Of his illness, he wrote,

> My life is but half done and I must leave it all.... All night I moaned; it was like being torn apart by lions. Delirious, I chattered like a swallow and moaned like a dove; my eyes grow weary of looking up for help. "O God," I cried, "I am in trouble—help me." But what can I say? For He Himself has sent this sickness. All my sleep has fled because of my soul's bitterness. O Lord, your discipline is good and leads to life and health. Oh, heal me and make me live! [Isaiah 38:10, 13–16 TLB]

And then, *after* his healing, the words

> Dead men cannot praise you. They cannot be filled with hope and joy. The living, only the living, can praise you and do today. One generation makes known your faithfulness to the next. Think of it! The Lord healed me! Every day of my life from now on I will sing my songs of praise in the temple, accompanied by the orchestra. [Isaiah 38:18–20 TLB]

There is a fine line, however, between masochism and deep worship for God that arises out of the depths. Sitting by the bedside of a very sick friend who was in deep pain, I heard her say, over and over, "The Lord is so good, so good." She was not thanking God for her suffering but rather she was praising him for sustenance and peace in the midst of her pain. Praise in the midst of pain is possible. I would not omit pain from my life if I could go back and do so, for out of it has come growth. But when I was in the pain I didn't like it one bit. One principle, therefore, of using suffering in order to grow is to submit to God's hand in it, to allow him to use it and to avoid resentment. But certainly we are not asked to enjoy it or like it.

Pain isolates the sufferer in the sense that no other human being can entirely share it. For no matter how much a person is loved, no one else can get inside of his or her skin and totally feel what he or she is feeling. Even with the most commonly experienced pain, like a toothache or headache, there is the human tendency to feel that no one has suffered in quite the same way before. Particularly isolating, however, is psychological pain, which seems genuinely unique, such as loss of a boyfriend or girlfriend or fear of old age. The isolation is obvious: Because most people have not experienced the trauma, they will not give it the same understanding that they give a toothache.

Not long ago, a friend of mine died in a car accident with his wife and two of his three children. John was young and had a bright future ahead of him in writing and Christian education. The children were all pre-adolescent, with their whole lifetimes ahead of them. One drunk truck driver ended all those futures, and a twelve-year-old boy was left as the sole survivor.

The night after the funeral I sat in my apartment talking to a friend, trying to comprehend what it would feel like to lose four family members in one day. I have lost four relatives in three years, and that has been difficult. I could barely imagine two losses at one time. Twelve-year-old Scott was offered comfort on all sides, but in a sense he was very isolated because no one he knew had ever experienced such a loss.

On a much smaller scale, we all feel alone in our pain at times. I think such emotions of aloneness are experienced by the alcoholic whose friends don't drink, the impotent man who feels he can't discuss the problem, or the elderly person who begins to feel his or her loss of sharpness of mind or vigor of body. While these problems are common, they are not so common that those so suffering feel free to talk to just anyone. And isolation increases the pain. A woman I know gives a good example in a poem that she wrote describing her feeling about the baby she always longed for and never had.

> Surely I gave you life!
> If only built on dreams and want—
> That was enough to spur you on your way.
> Did not the hours through all these years
> Time my laborious agonies?
> And have I not borne well the pain?
> Why, then, have I deserved you not?
>
> Has not my mind's womb held you—
> Turning, as you were, upon the axis of desire?
> Has not some distant bell clocked through the nights
> Your swift descent into reality?

> How often have I traced your course across my dreams!
> Oh, how I fancied your silk-brushed skull
> Against my cheeks,
> And felt my fingertips caught
> In the velvet creases of your hands
> Opening and closing with all the helplessness
> Of wanting to be real.
> Where are you?
> Still-born before you were conceived;
> Dust of my dreaming,
> Dust, in the tomb of my want.[4]

When she first read it to me I, being single and having had such feelings, was near tears. Another woman, also single, told me later, "I've never felt that way." She found the feelings impossible to relate to.

The greater the pain and the greater the isolation that it creates, the more important it is to find a meaning in suffering. I could not help the people I help nor have as great a freedom to write if I had children. Yet there are times when the choice of remaining single has hurt. But because none of us can have everything we want in this world, and because I find pleasure and purpose in my chosen lifestyle, the hurt of not having children does not make me bitter, just somewhat wistful at times.

Ultimately, there is no complete human answer to the problem of pain. We can understand it enough to comfort and be comforted. But the problem of pain remains a major philosophical question. It also provides a major challenge to trust God when we cannot see.

Such trust can be frightening at times, since most of us

prefer to see what is ahead. Yet trust need not be frightening when we realize God's love for us. The human conflict between trust and fear is graphically portrayed in an example from C. S. Lewis. C. W. Lewis says,

> A modern example may be found (if we are not too proud to see it there) in *The Wind in the Willows* when Rat and Mole approach Pan on the island.
> " 'Rat,' he found the breath to whisper, shaking, 'Are you afraid?' 'Afraid?' murmured the Rat, his eyes shining with unutterable love. 'Afraid? Of Him? O never, never. And yet—and yet—O Mole, I am afraid.' "[5]

Lewis goes on to present simple, graphic, but realistic answers to why we suffer. After describing a time of suffering and how he found through it that "all these toys were never intended to possess my heart, that my true good is in another world and my only real treasure is Christ,"[6] Lewis continues, "God has had me for but forty-eight hours and then only by dint of taking everything else away from me. Let Him but sheathe that sword for a moment and I behave like a puppy when the hated bath is over—I shake myself as dry as I can and race off to reacquire my comfortable dirtiness, if not in the nearest manure heap, at least in the nearest flower bed. And that is why tribulations cannot cease until God either sees us remade or sees that our remaking is now hopeless."[7]

There is great truth to what Lewis says. And, although God often refines his greatest servants with the hottest flames of affliction, we could perhaps eliminate some of the pain by more quickly learning that lesson of total commitment to Him. Greater pain for greater growth—

yet less pain the more quickly those divine lessons are learned. Paradoxical, certainly. Yet much of God is paradoxical, and we humans do God and ourselves a great injustice when we try to find our philosophical answers by oversimplifying God's truths.

Ultimately, Amy Carmichael may come closest to the truth when she says,

> Beautiful words do not satisfy the soul that is confined in the cell whose very substance is pain.... What, then, is the answer? I do not know. I believe that it is one of the secret things of the Lord, which will not be opened to us til we see Him who endured the Cross, see the scars in His hands and feet and side, see Him, our Beloved, face to face. I believe that in that revelation of love, which is far past our understanding now, we shall "understand even as all along we have been understood.
>
> And til then? What does a child do whose mother or father allows something to be done which it cannot understand? There is only one way of peace. It is the child's way. The loving child trusts.
>
> I believe that we who know our God, and have proved Him good past telling, will find rest there. The faith of the child rests on the character it knows. So may ours; so shall ours. Our Father does not explain, nor does He assure us as we long to be assured. For example, there is no word that I can find in the Bible that tells us that the faithful horse, which man's cruelty has maimed, will be far more than caused to forget on some celestial meadow; the dog betrayed far more than reassured; or that the little anguished child will be gathered in its angel's arms and there far more than comforted. But we know Our Father. We know His character. Somehow, somewhere, the wrong must be put

right; *how* we do not know, only we know that, because He is what He is anything else is inconceivable. For the word sent to the man whose soul was among lions and who was soon to be done to death, unsuccored, though the Lord of Daniel was so near, is fathomless: "And blessed is he whosoever shall not be offended in me."[8]

Once when I lay ill for two weeks in bed, I was having a difficult time of it. How silly that sounded to me even then, when so many people spend their lives sick and in bed. This thought did not alleviate my pain, however, and I find that to remind patients others suffer more than they do creates anger, not comfort.

On this particular occasion, my doctor was not completely certain of how to treat me (which is often the case in metabolic disorders). He could give me no guarantee of when I might return to work, and he was overly sympathetic, increasing the self-pity I was temporarily tempted to allow.

Weak from a very low blood pressure, I lay in bed and thought. Why when I had so much to do—good things at that—did I have to be sick? And why now? My patients needed me, and several were either new or very disturbed. Furthermore, it had been a difficult year. I was tired of pain, and I could feel my anger at God developing. It was quite obvious that I could fuss and fume myself into greater illness and spiritual loss or I could *choose* to make my experience usable both to myself and to others.

My prayer was simple: "Forgive me for wanting my own way. Thank you for all You've done in the past, and take over completely. Do with me and in me what you want from this experience of pain. And, dear God, please do comfort me in Your own way." Our Lord must smile at the last sentence of such a prayer, but I believe he also answers and understands.

With an act of faith designed to keep me diverted from thinking any more about my situation, I slowly got out of bed, put on my bathing suit, and went out to continue my rest by the pool. It was one of those rare warm spring days in February with which those of us who live in California are sometimes blessed. I sank down wearily on the towel, thanking God for the warmth of the sun. Then I opened a book of Amy Carmichael's, an author to whom I often turn when I need courage or comfort.

> Thunder clouds are nothing to the Spirit of Joy. The only special reference to the joy of the Holy Spirit is bound up with the words "much affliction," much pressure.
>
> "Joy is not gush; joy is not jolliness. Joy is simply perfect acquiescence in God's will, because the soul delights itself in God Himself."[9]

The seal on my decision to trust God with a total abandonment came as I read her concluding words to the chapter:

> Make me thy mountaineer;
> I would not linger on a lower slope.
> Fill me afresh with hope, O God of hope,
> That undefeated I may climb the hill
> As seeing Him who is invisible.[10]

"I would not linger on a lower slope." I would not waste this opportunity to trust God, to watch him work out my circumstances. I would not waste this suffering.

Once again I was conscious of the sun's warmth and now of the clear blue sky overhead—a rarity in Los Angeles! I was still weak. I still thought about my patients. There would be moments of testing and doubt about my health. But I was safe, for I had chosen to put my trust in the God who cannot fail. And, in some almost unconscious way, that kind of commitment gave me a deep sense of worth. Not only had I acted positively in my pain, but the God of all the universe was acting on my behalf.

NOTES

1. Joseph B. Fabry, *The Pursuit of Meaning* (Boston: Beacon Press, 1968), p. 45.
2. Fabry (1968), pp. 44–45.
3. Fabry (1968), p. 49.
4. Dianne Neval, *Fantasis 1* (1947, unpublished).
5. *The Problem of Pain*, C. S. Lewis, (New York: Macmillan, 1962), p. 18.
6. Lewis (1962), p. 106.
7. Lewis (1962), p. 107.
8. Amy Carmichael, *Rose From Brier* (London: Society for Promoting Christian Knowledge, 1933), pp. 198–199.
9. Amy Carmichael, *Gold by Moonlight* (Great Britain: Christian Literature Crusade, undated), pp. 74–75.
10. Carmichael (undated), p. 75.

CHAPTER 6

In Respect to Caring

A thirty-year-old woman, Chris, felt her marriage was ending and sought help from the minister of her church. They had several good sessions, and then they disagreed. The pastor felt that Chris's basic problem with her father must be resolved before she could relate to her husband. He suggest that she go to her father, confess her lack of love, and develop a relationship.

For Chris, such confrontation seemed almost impossible. Her father had been an alcoholic for as long as she could remember. She had been sexually molested by him when she was eight and again when she was thirteen. At sixteen, she was told to "get out and make your own living." Then, after living in foster homes for two years, she had met Ed, her husband.

She had forgiven her father because she felt that such an act was imperative if she was to function fully as a

Christian. But a relationship? How many times she had tried to form one and had been rebuffed and rejected! Now her pastor was telling her that she was sinning until that relationship was developed, that indeed her whole marriage depended on it. What was even more confusing was the fact that Chris could see no connection between Ed and her relationship with her father. Ed never wanted her to see her father. He felt that such an encounter would be disastrous. Furthermore, problems with Ed centered around his affair with another woman, not her relationship with her father. Did she need added pain right now? With that thought, Chris had left the pastoral chambers and ended up in my office. She felt not only the rejection by her husband but also that by the church and a renewal of the pain caused by her father's lack of love!

When the pastor of Chris's church called me a few days later, he was obviously a little nervous about his image. In detail, he repeated what he had said and defended it. Then he lost his cool. "She's just spoiled," he blurted out. "She needs to learn to submit." I politely got off the phone.

A basic function of the church is to build up its various members, emotionally as well as in every other way. The church should nourish the self-esteem of its members. Deadness and legalism are two primary roadblocks to the effective building of good self-esteem.

We live in an era of "disposable friends." We put down our roots into any relationship with a guarded sense of shallowness because we might lose that relationship to a new job in a new city. We live in an era of changing ideas, rapid communication, and intensive research, so that at times we find our beliefs challenged and fluctuating within a very short span of time. Such an emotional climate militates against the long-standing type of security that people formerly received from the organized church, for the church, too, is mobile, with a rapidly changing membership. The result is often a dead, ineffective church with a congregation who seek to meet their emotional needs elsewhere.

Susan was a pretty, eighteen-year-old girl who was very much alone in the world. Her starting salary at a dress shop was good, but not good enough to pay for an apartment, food and psychological help, too. Yet she needed and wanted to get competent help in solving problems which have deep roots in her personality.

The therapist she chose was one of the best and reasonably expensive. Yet because he was so well qualified, therapy with him could have turned out to be cheaper than a longer term of treatment with someone else.

The problem was money. One evening we sat down and figured out all of her expenses and income. The result was more encouraging than we had anticipated. If she did not do much but eat, work and sleep, she only needed twenty-five dollars more a month.

With considerable enthusiasm we decided to look for a part-time job for her. Two days later I learned of a secretarial job in a local church. The hours were good. Pay was acceptable. And it was the perfect chance to get Susan involved in a church where Christ was presented. There she could experience real Christian love.

Susan called. A woman with a cold, efficient voice said, "I'm sorry I put that ad in the paper right now. I'm too busy to answer the phone."

Figuring it must have been just a bad day for her, Susan asked about the job. Yes, she said she would hire Susan, but only to try her out. She didn't like someone young. She had had a bad experience before with a teenager.

The following week, Susan appeared at the church and worked hard. She got along well with the other, older volunteers and like the work. But the lady remained aloof. At the end of the morning she told Susan that she would try out other people and let her know in several weeks.

Susan had neither the reward of a permanent job offer nor the courtesy of a definite turn-down. She was neither commended nor corrected. And the lady never called back.

A few weeks later, Susan found the kind of love I had hoped she would find in the church. Needing immediate medical care for a broken arm and not having the money to pay for it, she went to a local clinic that treats people who cannot afford to pay. It is located in an area heavily populated by young drug addicts, homosexuals and runaways. Many of the best doctors in the Los Angeles area donate time. Accountants, secretaries and people from other walks of life volunteer as nurses to help the doctors.

No one in the clinic preached Christ. No one claimed to have had his life transformed by the love of God. But that night they showed love to a lonely teenager who had not found it in church a few weeks before. As she put it, they showed her respect.[1]

Respect! That is a key word in a good self-image. Surely as Christians we are obligated to respect one another, to treat another as our equal, as worthy of love. But in the countless hundreds of churches across this country, held together by dogma that has lost its meaning for many and lacking the reality of "Christ in me," twentieth-century stress has been the final death blow to the effectiveness of the organized church.

And for those churches who have retained meaning and even deep spiritual relationships within their group, too often there has been a clinging to legalism as a point of safety in the middle of an age of tremendous change. This, too, is lethal to real progress in building up the members of a church. A legalistic emphasis on rules is hardly ever a revelation of real spiritual truth. Rather, it is a matter of holding on to rules and ideas without considering their validity. It is holding to the extreme in order to militate against the pain of change in a society that has been inundated with excessive change. It is easier to make rules about conduct and dress than it is to change attitudes and develop relationships. Change can be painful because it is new. And new is scary. But, when we change our lives into something better, it is worth the pain.

I recently talked to a patient who had just begun to accept anger within herself. Paradoxically, she said, "I feel so much better and in control of my life now that I can begin to handle my anger. Now at least I don't throw my anger at everyone or give up and get depressed. But still it's been scary just seeing myself as an angry person!" Her experience of change has been liberating, while her old attitude of legalism, which in her case made her feel that anger was a sin, was crippling.

God's balance is somewhere in the middle: holding on to what one believes is true because it is true and changing when change produces new truth or new application of old truths. Legalism by itself, without spiritual reality, turns people away from the church as much or more than spiritual deadness. Both isolate people from entering into fellowship with other believers who can mutually build each other up.

I know of a man, unethical in his business dealings and slanderous with his tongue, who will not engage in fellowship with a fellow Christian who drinks or smokes. I know of Christians who cannot tolerate a member of the church who is in psychotherapy or who forever repudiates those involved in an extramarital affair. These Christians extend themselves for no one, while their friends with all the "problems" are struggling to change, to grow, to become what they were meant to be. Who really has the greater problem?

C. S. Lewis, using ethics as an example, beautifully portrays Christian balance:

> While the rule of chastity is the same for all Christians at all times, the rule of propriety changes. A girl in the Pacific islands wearing hardly any clothes and a Victorian lady completely covered in clothes might both be equally "modest," proper, or decent, according to the standards of their own societies; and both, for all we could tell by their dress, might be equally chaste (or equally unchaste).[2]

Lewis continues,

> I think that old, or old-fashioned, people should be very careful not to assume that young or 'emancipated' people

are corrupt whenever they are (by the old standard) improper; and, in return, that young people should not call their elders prudes or puritans because they do not easily adopt the new standard. A real desire to believe all the good you can of others and to make others as comfortable as you can will solve most of the problems.[3]

If we were really trying to believe the best and to make each other comfortable, we would be effective agents in raising each other's self-images. But a deadness that has no spiritual commitment or a legalism involving only a shallow endorsement of rules will not lead into relationships that, while not always in agreement, will be vital and uplifting.

In his book *The Whole Person in a Broken World*, Paul Tournier summarizes well the position of the organized church:

> Our age is suffering because of the rift between the spiritual and the temporal. It is suffering not only because of the despiritualization of the world, but also because of the disincarnation of the church. The church, it seems to me, has separated itself from real life and thus simply abandoned the world to its practical difficulties and taken refuge in an ivory tower. And for this it bears a heavy responsibility for our present crisis. True, it still goes on preaching, but far from the public place where the practical life of men is lived. "Morality is not a theory which one proves," writes Dr. Zeviekl, "but rather a life that one demonstrates by living." And then, speaking of all the social and intellectual struggles that throbbed within his heart and mind, he goes on to say: "My generation, which was shaped and matured between the two world wars . . . was dominated above all by

political movements which were for the most part far removed from Christianity." The world in which he lived was "a world in which Jesus was absent." I am reminded also of what Peguy said about Christians: "Their hands are clean, but they have no hands."[4]

The existence of these inconsistencies, as well as the existence of much trivia within church meetings, tends to cause Christians to operate at times in much greater isolation than did the New Testament church. C. S. Lewis states his feelings about churchgoing with greater bluntness than most of us could muster.

He first describes his reluctant conversion after a long period of slowly coming to God, or as he would state it, God coming to Lewis:

> You must picture me alone in that room in Magdalen, night after night, feeling, whenever my mind lifted even for a second from my work, the steady unrelenting approach of Him whom I so earnestly desired not to meet. That which I greatly feared had at last come upon me. In the Trinity Term of 1929 I gave in, and admitted that God was God, and knelt and prayed: Perhaps that night, the most dejected and reluctant convert in all of England. I did not then see what is now the most shining and obvious thing; the Divine humility which will accept a convert even on such terms. The Prodigal Son at least walked home on his own feet. But who can duly adore that Love which will open the high gates to a prodigal who is brought in kicking, struggling, resentful and darting his eyes in every direction for a chance to escape?[5]

And then Lewis continues,

> The idea of churchmanship was to me wholly unattractive. It was, to begin with, a kind of collective; a wearisome "get-together" affair. I couldn't yet see how a concern of that sort should have anything to do with one's spiritual life. To me, religion ought to have been a matter of good men praying alone and meeting by twos and threes to talk of spiritual matters. And the fussy time-wasting botheration of it all! the bells, the crowds, the umbrellas, the notices, the bustle, the perpetual arranging and organizing. Hymns were (and are) extremely disagreeable to me. Of all the musical instruments I liked (and like) the organ least. I have, too, a sort of spiritual *gaucherie* which makes me unapt to participate in any rite.
>
> Thus my churchgoing was a merely symbolic and provisional practice. If it in fact helped to move me in the Christian direction, I was and am unaware of this."[6]

In contrast, the New Testament church played an integral part in building up its various members. Widows were cared for—physically, even financially! The ill were prayed over. Those who sinned were forgiven and restored. Growth occurred. The church met daily at first and then weekly to celebrate the sacrament of the Lord's Supper. Here was a church who knew and valued worship. There was biblical teaching, both from traveling and local teachers. Members ate together, and when traveling they stayed in each other's homes. Churchgoing was not just "a wearisome 'get-together' affair."

Such a church is biblical. In the New Testament, the

church is portrayed by the image of a body with all its various members. Any local church that exists is just a part of the total church, the body of Christ. And, just as a body functions with each part playing a vital part in connection with the whole, so each member in the church is to contribute to and be affected by each other member.

I Corinthians 12 (TLB) reads:

> Our bodies have many parts, but the many parts make up only one body when they are all put together. So it is with the "body" of Christ [12]
>
> Yes, the body has many parts, not just one part. If the foot says, "I am not a part of the body because I am not a hand," that does not make it any less a part of the body. And what would you think if you heard an ear say, "I am not part of the body because I am only an ear, and not an eye"? Suppose the whole body were an eye—then how would you hear? Or if your whole body were just one big ear, how could you smell anything? [14–17]
>
> But that isn't the way God has made us. He has made many parts for our bodies and has put each part just where he wants it. What a strange thing a body would be if it had only one part! So He has made many parts, but still there is only one body. [18–20]
>
> The eye can never say to the hand, "I don't need you." The head can't say to the feet, "I don't need you." [21]
>
> And some of the parts that seem weakest and least important are really the most necessary. Yes, we are especially glad to have some parts that seem rather odd! And we carefully protect from the eyes of others those parts that should not be seen, while of course the parts that may be seen do not require this special care. So God has put the body to-

gether in such a way that extra honor and care are given to those parts that might otherwise seem less important. This makes for happiness among the parts, so that the parts have *the same care for each other that they do for themselves.* If one part suffers, all parts suffer with it, and if one part is honored, all the parts are glad. [22–26]

As I was finishing a manuscript, I needed some last quiet moments—and a lot of help—in order to complete my work on time. A friend and I went to the beach, where I rented a cabin. I was able to give her a week at the ocean. She cooked and ran errands. Another friend called long distance because he hoped I was doing well as the week drew toward its end. Another friend came down for two days and typed for me. Interrelatedly, we helped each other with the skills and time that we possessed. And each person involved felt a greater sense of worth for what he or she gave and received in the relationship.

On a superficial level, this is what the church is to be doing. On a deeper level, one must consider all of the gifts of the spirit that are listed, like teaching, prophecy, healing, miracles, wisdom, faith, tongues. All of these indicate the deep capacity which the church has to minister to its members.

But the bottom line in a church that functions in such a way as to truly foster a good self image among its members is contained in one word—*love.* We read in I Corinthians 12:2 that no spiritual gift has value without love. One cannot mitigate the power of that word *nothing.* "If I had the gift of faith so that I could speak to a mountain and make it move, I would still be worth *nothing at all without love.*" For it is love that spreads to another human being as water is received by dry, parched soil and revives that person's being, making him or her feel that he or she is truly a person of worth. One little girl summed up the value of love very succinctly when she said, "I don't want to be a Christian like my mother but like my sister. She loves people."

But Gibran was correct when he said that work is love made visible. And so, in evangelical circles where works are shied away from because we're saved by faith, we need to stop fearing a faith that issues forth into works. The other half of justification by faith is that faith without works is dead. In our deadness, we too often have become truly a church without hands. And so we neither love nor are loved. We neither extend ourselves in worthwhile deeds nor are extended to.

Sometimes Christians come to me for counseling, not because their problems require professional help, but because they're afraid even to admit to their fellow church members and Christian friends that they *have* problems. At this point, they actually pay for love and acceptance. There is a place in Christianity for professional psychological help that is valid and used of God in the healing of a damaged self-image. But for those who stumble or hurt and merely need a loving hand to pick them up the church is responsible—and failing.

To love means to put aside your own tastes and biases. It does not mean that you agree with what you hear but that you still tolerate and love the person who states the offending idea. It means a curious combination of toughness and gentleness. It means being unshockable. What destroys the power of the church more? Adultery or gossip? Drug addiction or unlove? Alcoholism or dishonesty in business? Jesus Christ was unshockable as he ate with those who were known sinners. He gave them a sense of their worth to him. But he was extremely intolerant of religious hypocrisy and lack of love.

An old hymn I learned in college states the issue well:

> For the love of God is broader
> than the measures of man's mind
> and the heart of the Eternal
> is most wonderfully kind.
>
> But we make His love too narrow
> by false limits of our own
> And we magnify its strictness
> with a zeal He will not own.

We look at Charles Manson and his followers critically—and we should. But with our love would there ever be a Charles Manson? As he said at his trial, "Most of the people at the ranch that you call the 'family' were just people that you did not want, people that were alongside the road. Their parents kicked them out so I did the best I could and took them on my garbage dump."[7]

In a hospital bed, an old man lay dying of an unknown disease that had baffled the staff. "He's senile," said one doctor. "He doesn't understand what we're doing." Then as they roughly tore off his sheet and began to examine him, he resisted them, and they gave up defeated and disgruntled. A nurse watched the scene quietly and waited until the doctors left. She put the man's teeth back into his mouth so that he could talk, and she spoke warmly to him. She treated him as if he were *not* senile, and she found out that indeed he was not impaired in any way intellectually. Finally he explained his uncooperativeness. It was simple. He didn't like being examined rudely and roughly. He wanted the dignity of an explanation. She talked with him for a while and then, at the staff meeting, explained his feelings. I was in the hall when the head doctor came out. "I guess we'll have to explain each step," he said in an irritated tone of voice. Yet the result of that nurse's concern was cooperativeness by the patient, which led to better treatment; an easier time for the physicians, who didn't have to fight the patient's resistance; and a patient who had regained his self-respect. Sometimes a little love will go a long way.

The church has within its power the greatest tool in raising self-esteem—the power of the love of Jesus Christ. It can sit in indifference and complain about the way the world is deteriorating. It can concern itself only with its own needs. Or each member of that church, the body of Christ, can function in love for a world that sometimes forgets what real love even feels like.

In his book *The Mountain People,* Colin Turnbull describes the culture of the Ik, who have lost all love. One of the men in the tribe awakened to find his family huddled by the fire, cold and hungry.

> He gave out a cry of despair that he turned to poetry and to song, asking how God could allow such unhappiness and

misery to those he had let down from the sky; asking why He had retreated beyond their reach, leaving them without hope. He sang to himself and his wife and children for half an hour, and then fell into a silence that was even more bitter than the song.

For all around were others who were also cold and hungry, but who had lost all trust in the world, had lost all love and all hope, who merely accepted life's brutality and cruelty because it was empty of all else. They had no love left that could be tortured and compelled to express itself as grief, and no God to sing to, for they were Ik.[8]

Christian love or the world of the Ik? Extremes? Perhaps, but we too are becoming a self-centered society who know less and less of real love. To love is to reach outside of oneself. And love is essential in the development of self-worth. The Iks once knew love of some kind. They too had family ties. They too extended themselves. They too felt a sense of worth. Then in one generation they lost it all. I recently drove down a major street in Los Angeles and observed a man lying unconscious on the sidewalk. Ten minutes later, when I got to a phone and called for help, I discovered that no one else had called before me. I began to wonder if we too are not turning inward and forgetting to love.

The Bible is accurate. Without love, we have nothing. And, I would add, without love one feels a great deficit of self-worth. Only in the midst of great love do we accept ourselves and grow into a sense of ever-deepening self-worth.

NOTES

1. Elizabeth Skoglund, *Can I Talk to You?* (Glendale, Calif.: Regal Books Division, G/L Publications, 1977, pp. 141–142.
2. C. S. Lewis, *Mere Christianity* (London: Collins Clear-Type Press, 1952). p. 84.
3. Lewis (1952), p. 85.
4. Paul Tournier, *The Whole Person in a Broken World* (New York: Harper & Row, 1964), pp. 159–160.
5. C. S. Lewis, *Surprised by Joy* (New York: Harcourt, Brace & Co, 1955), opp. 228–229.
6. Lewis (1955), pp. 233–234.
7. *Los Angeles Herald Examiner*, November 22, 1970, p. A-7, col. 3.
8. Colin Turnbull, *The Mountain People* (New York: Simon & Schuster, 1972), p. 264.

CHAPTER 7

Survival Zone in a Changing World

Flying at dusk from the Mexico City airport to a small coastal town, I felt like I was being thrust into another world, another era of time for a brief period. We were a little late. No one else seemed concerned. There were six of us on the plane, all speaking Spanish except for me. A lady across the aisle quietly began to nurse her baby, and a small boy tried to sell me a newspaper I couldn't read.

I turned back to look at the lady with the small infant. I watched her as she tenderly stroked the child's face. Her eyes gazed admiringly at the tiny hands that clutched at her clothes. She and the baby were absorbed in each other, and each appeared content. I wondered who this child would be when he grew up. Perhaps he would be too poor to get an education. Maybe poverty would limit his whole life. On the other hand, with the abundance of love that was apparently his, a good self-image might also be his and could well be valued above the fortunes that most people so frantically seek.

That night in the small village, my impressions were further deepened. Houses without walls, dogs with only bones showing through their skin, people living and dying within a small radius of where they were born; it very remote from the world I knew.

Yet the next day, as I saw children treated lovingly and as I fidgeted in the afternoon sun, looking for something to do, and watched everyone else sleeping peacefully through the heat, I wondered again how much these people were really missing. In the short time I was there, my own expectations, to put it into Thomas Carlyle's words, were reduced to zero. I didn't miss modern conveniences that much. Ice cubes, pure water, the ocean, and good friends seemed all that were essential. Yet too much of today's world is instilled in me for me to forever leave my work and ambition for even this tropical paradise. And so as I returned to this country and deadlines and schedules, Wordsworth's shades of the prison house began to close in, and I entered the world of Toffler's *Future Shock*.

What was so deeply significant to me in Mexico was the fact that I *did* notice a difference, not only in lifestyles but also in the effect of those lifestyles on my self-image. At home, I rushed. I always seemed to finish my work, but at such a pace! And I felt the pressure of my friends: their frustration over constant change, their inability to cope. As a therapist, in particular, I observed the confused values and feelings of worthlessness that prevail among so many. In Mexico, at least I felt calm. Perhaps it was partly because it was new and different. Still, they had something in their simplification of life that made them vastly different from us.

Mobility and increased communication are two major differences. We move around a lot, and so we lose and gain friends quickly. Last year three close friends of mine moved. They certainly weren't rejecting me, but I did feel somewhat abandoned.

Additionally, in my particular lifestyle of counseling and writing it is at times hard to get away from demands and ringing phones in order to write or to just get back into touch with myself.

Nor are my experiences unique. A pastor I know never tries to write even in his study at church. A housewife turns off the phones when she *must* have just a few moments to herself. A college student has stopped watching television news because "Who needs to know all about the recent murders around the country?"

To a smaller or greater degree, people who are affected by our increase in mobility and communication feel a shakiness about themselves. Moving, or having those we love move, isolates. And self-images are nourished by relationships, not by isolation. Running from telephone calls may protect our time alone, but it also prevents us from hearing from people who do love us and build us up. Even the media causes problems. If we watch it too much, we feel the whole world is truly in terrible shape. If we don't watch it, we again feel isolated and out of touch.

Such problems are not easy to solve but they are solvable. Structuring heads the list of solutions. There are times when I need a block of two or three days to write. Often I go to the ocean and stay there. I simply tell my family my plans, leave my telephone number, and go. (I'm not married, so I can get by with that!)

If someone doesn't understand or sarcastically remarks that "I've joined the jet set," I have to deal with my own self-image problems, not theirs. And just because someone who does not write does not understand me should not offset my view of myself. Conversely, when my family or friends who have adolescent children fly into the dark some night for a two-week break, I can understand their needs even though I've never had them.

Each of us feels that his or her problems are unique. No one has ever felt quite like we do. Yet, as I sit in my office and hear patients pour out their problems about their inner feelings, I find *no* one is unique in the quantity of his or her pain. Many people suffer deeply, and, while each is different from the next, there are great areas of commonality. We feel put down when someone thinks we're overreacting to a situation. But we also put people down when we do the same to them. In this age of mass movement of people and thoughts, we do well to accept and fulfill our needs in responsible ways that we can work out and to allow others to do the same.

Structuring varies from person to person. A woman

with four children—ages two months to five years—is not a prima donna for hiring someone to clean her house. She's buying time—time to retain her own identity. The physician who takes four two-week vacations a year is preserving his or her health and building his or her self-image by, in essence, saying, "I'm worth preserving." A lady I know marks her TV guide with a special program to watch every evening so that no matter how harried the day gets she takes something for herself. Women's magazines now have articles recommending bathing by candlelight with a cup of coffee or a glass of wine—with music of course. It's a good idea, and it can work.

Setting up some kind of stability zone is another form of structuring. A cup of coffee, or two, is essential as a first thing in the morning routine for me. Without it, the day starts all wrong. Something quiet, like a Psalm, or a novel, or a nonsensical thing like an old movie are all good for me at night. A friend of mine plays golf every Saturday. It is as much a part of his week as his work, and it feeds his needs. I suppose tea in the afternoon was, or is, a stability zone for the British. Some people do needlework. A neighbor walks her dog two miles. Another works out at the YMCA. No matter how trivial, a routine that we count on and that is enjoyable helps ameliorate the instability of the pace and change around us.

Self-hypnosis, yoga, the after-work drink, clothes-buying sprees and deep breathing are all "in" because true freedom and a slowed-down pace are "out" as far as the reality of our age is concerned. Maybe that's why Mexico appealed to me. One didn't need self-hypnosis and deep breathing in order to relax. But in our society one can only face the problems of pace that exist, handle them within a workable structure for us, and realize that much of our inner frustration arises not so much from how badly we plan our lives but from the demands of change and trauma that infringe on them.

However, pace, mobility, communication—these are not the only twentieth-century problems that threaten our sense of worth. On at least as deep a level are the issues of ethics, morale, and even the very definition of "What is a worthwhile person?" At the root of our confusion is, once again, fast change. When I was in high school, virginity was considered a virtue. Now it is unusual and even suspect. Similarly, twenty years ago, all acceptable women were married. Now, marriage is okay but certainly not essential. Singleness is more than ever acceptable as a viable lifestyle. Women can do men's jobs, and men can do women's work. Yet the real "in" thing to have is the best of both worlds: the man who can be gentle and changes diapers, and also he has a regular job as a policeman; or the woman executive who dresses seductively and is a gourmet cook.

At times, the change around us can become deeply destructive to those who indulge it. The man I saw who traded wives with his best friend, "just for a night," was deeply hurt when his own wife made love with his best friend! The forty-year-old woman who went to the mountains for a weekend of fun and ended up "trying a homosexual experience because it was a new feeling" came into therapy with a really confused view of who she was. Nor did she know how to handle the guilt she felt about her husband. Such cultural confusion is not only true of non-Christians, for I have heard the same stories from Christians as well. One thing you learn in a therapist's office is that Christians are as human as anyone else. And, Christian or not, we are all affected to some degree by the changes around us.

Some of the changes are good, some questionable or bad. But they are all fast changes, requiring reactions from people who may already not be too sure of themselves.

Add to this dilemma the question of "Who is worthwhile?" or "What is worth?" and the issue becomes still further complicated. Ethel Waters died recently and, from what I understand, had great physical problems at the end and no money except what she received from Social Security. She came from a poor family. She rose to the top in the secular entertainment world. She excelled later in the Christian world, particularly in her frequent appearances at Billy Graham crusades. Because of what she did for God, and presumably because of the kind of person she was, Ethel Waters had worth. But what about money and fame? Does one have to have both to be successful? If not, is it better to be famous and die poor or not famous and die rich? Or is power greater than either fame or wealth? I'm not sure we have answers to such questions from the view point of society, because these values are still changing and unstable.

It is at this point that biblical principles become greatly stabilizing. While the Bible gives specific commands relating to life situations, it is also very basically a book of general principles to be applied specifically in every age and culture.

For mobility, there is the God that changes not and is ever-present. For the traumatic impact of communication through mass media, there is the God who is in total control of all life events and who protects his own. In sexual mores, the Bible is timeless in its specific wisdom of purity and relationships bound together for all eternity rather than for a fleeting moment of gratification. For changing sexual roles, there is the biblical distinctiveness of the sexes with greater internal fluidity than is generally noted. The gentleness of the Master as he washed his disciples feet and the leadership of Deborah as she led Barek to war are as biblical as the roles of husbands and wives as defined in Ephesians 6. And as to the primary question, "What is worth?" the Bible is most clear. Moses left the luxury of his life as ths king's son to lead Israel out of Egypt; Joseph lay in a prison cell because of his virtue in resisting his supervisor's wife. Job, bereft of all of his fortune, said, "Though He slay me yet will I trust Him." Abraham believed he would be given a son long after Sarah could naturally bear that son. A rich man gave his own tomb for the burial of Jesus Christ. Priscilla and Aquilla quietly taught Barnabas in the first-century church. These were people of worth. A worth summarized by the life of David, who in his life of service committed both adultery and murder, but who was called by God "A man after my own heart." In whatever the circumstance or culture, to be a person after God's own heart is to have great worth. It is stabilizing not to have to worry about financial status, power, fame, but instead to concern oneself over one question: "In this life I am living, and I a person after God's own heart?" This concept simplifies. It clarifies. And it makes every person a potential winner.

Perhaps one group of people above all others in this society show the strain of not knowing their worth. That group are those people in so-called Christian work: ministers, heads of Christian organizations, and missionaries. Some hide physical disabilities that might reflect on their efficiency in the running of an organization. Many conceal bad marriages and unmanageable children. They must appear well off to be successful but not so well off as to be affluent. Unlike David, if they have sexual affairs, and they do, the organized church would rarely believe that they could ever again be men or women after God's own heart. When they are ill, they are considered to perhaps lack faith. But if their life is too smooth they perhaps are not men of God. We put them on pedestals and knock them down because we must have their perfection and then cannot bear to live with it after all.

And what we do to organized Christian workers, we do to ourselves. We dare not be human and yet be OK, not realizing that *no one* is OK unless his or her full desire is toward God. While it is true that what we do outwardly reflects our inward being, it is more the inward than the outward part that God evaluates.

The other night I lay in bed wondering how I could meet all my deadlines with writing and patients and still be myself. If I were rich, I could go away for a month and write. But I'm not rich, and, besides, patients need me. If I were just a therapist, I would not have to worry about writing deadlines. But I love writing. I tightened up. My muscles were taut and my brain spinning. Then came the ever-reassuring Word, speaking as that still quiet inner voice: "You are mine, and the work is mine." And I realized two things: how dispensable I am and how much God supplies in every way. Again it was F. B. Meyer's "Thy strength, Lord, Thy peace." And I slept.

The simplification of a life given to God, receiving God's supply and God's direction is so easy and yet so profound in the frantic day in which we live. It is eternally simple, profound, and true. And once again the key is a committment to that simplicity and, above all, to God.

A young girl in her early teens sat across from me in my office and told me of her conflict over such things as obedience to parents, sex, boyfriends, and drinking. We talked, but I could see that her best answers would come as she and God talked it out. Basically, she had been given so many different answers from Christians that she wasn't sure of anyone except God. She had attended a conference that emphasized obedience to parents on any issue at any age. And that had seemed extreme. Friends her own age seemed to have no stable answers, and so she analyzed and thought and at least once a week we talked.

Then one Saturday morning, she came to my office with a calmness I had not often seen in her. She had found her answer to all the fluctuating opinions around her. To my surprise, she had not adopted any of the extremes she had heard but, rather, had arrived at what I believe was a healthy balance. "For right now," she said, "at this time, I believe I should obey my parents. But that doesn't mean they're always right or that I will do all that they say when I'm twenty-five. But at thirteen it seems right." Most of her friends were disappointed. Some wanted her to always have her parents as the final authority. Others wanted her to totally rebel. Her conclusion was not altogether typical of the twentieth century, but it was biblical and I was proud of her.

In biblical terms, Moses also came to grips with his own cultural shock in a way that applies today. Moses, the man of mobility who traveled for forty years with the criticism of those who wanted the security of even Egypt, bad as that was, could say as he was dying,

> There is none like God....
> Who rides through the heavens to your help
> and in his majesty through the skies.
> The eternal God is your dwelling place,
> And underneath are the everlasting arms....
> So Israel dwelt in safety.
> [Deut. 33:26–28 RSV]

Herein is the stability of the person of God who makes Jehovah his standard and strength. Not flaunting without sense the ideas of his or her culture but in balance applying biblical principles to twentieth-century living.

"What then is man?" asks Viktor Frankl, and continues:

We have learned to know him, as possibly no generation before us. We have learned to know him in camps, where everything unessential has been stripped from man, where ev-

erything which a person had—money, power, fame, luck—disappeared: While only that remained which man does not "have" but which he must be." What remained was man himself, who in the white heat of suffering and pain was melted down to the essentials, to the human in himself.
What then is man? We ask again. He is a being who continually decides what he is: a being who equally harbors the potential to descend to the level of an animal or to ascend to the life of a saint. Man is that being, who, after all, invented the gas chambers, but at the same time he is that being who entered into those same gas chambers with his head held high and with "Our Father" or the Jewish prayer of the dying on his lips.[1]

This then is humanity. This today is still the essence of our worth.

NOTE

1. Viktor E. Frankl, *Psychotherapy and Existentialism* (New York: Simon & Schuster, 1967), p. 110.